the art of being a
LION

BARNES
&NOBLE
BOOKS
NEW YORK

TEXTS AND PHOTOGRAPHS
CHRISTINE & MICHEL DENIS-HUOT

HISTORICAL INTRODUCTION
GIANNI GUADALUPI

EDITORIAL DIRECTOR
VALERIA MANFERTO DE FABIANIS

GRAPHIC DESIGN
PATRIZIA BALOCCO LOVISETTI

TRANSLATION
KEVIN MACIEL-C.T.M., MILAN AND AMY EZRIN

CONTENTS

1
A lion cub of 4-5 months comes to nuzzle his mother after a nap.

2-3
In the cool night, lions recover all of their vigor. They may run up to 5 miles to catch their prey whereas during the day, they are exhausted after just a few yards.

4-5
On the edge of the marsh, a lioness of the Bila Shaka pride takes up position on a trunk, from where she can calmly observe the surroundings.

6
Detail of a funerary bed discovered in the tomb of Pharaoh Tutankhamun shows Mehet, goddess of destruction, who guarantees the floods of the Nile, according to the religion of Ancient Egypt.

7
A lioness stares at an approaching male in order to steal his prey.

© 2002 White Star S.r.l.
Via C. Sassone, 22/24
13100 Vercelli, Italy
www.whitestar.it

This edition published by
Barnes & Noble, Inc., by arrangement
with White Star S.r.l.
2003 Barnes & Noble Books

Library of Congress
Cataloging-in-Publication
Data available

ISBN 0-7607-4767-9
M10987654321

Printed in Singapore by Star Standard

PREFACE

8
The mane gives the male his majestic look.

9
It is time to begin the hunt. A big yawn signals the departure of the troupe.

10-11
After playing with his little friends, a lion cub finds a comfortable position to rest in.

We still consider the lion the king of animals, about whom legends have been built and buttressed over millennia of fables and folklore. A fascinating creature, like all the big cats, it inhabited the European landscape in prehistoric times. The cave lion was a contemporary of the Neanderthal and Cro-Magnon man.

A symbol of power, the lion is famous for its flamboyant mane, its noble carriage, the large amber eyes, and its powerful, blood-chilling roar. While Man has often envied its sexual prowess, in reality frequent mating is a biological necessity for the lion to ensure the survival of its species.

A predominantly nocturnal animal, the lion often seems slothful and lazy. But, does it really need to be more active? Dominating the savannah, the lion contemplates with noble indifference the species that surround it, all representing potential prey. It does not need to fear other predators, except Man who has hunted it for centuries. Today, lion populations survive only in the large nature parks and reserves of East Africa.

The lion is the only cat to live in groups within which tasks are shared on the basis of gender. Males fight to impose their dominance over a harem of females and their territory. They must then defend the pride against pretenders without a harem. Females are in charge of collectively bringing up cubs and hunting for food. The males then only have to help themselves to the feast. Despite its legendary majesty, the lion is also a pirate of the steppe who in lean times will not disdain carrion or hesitate before stooping to petty theft. Within the pride, everything runs smoothly so long as food is plentiful. Otherwise, only the strong eat. It is simply unfortunate for the young cubs who are no longer able to get their share of food. As all good things must, the lion's leisurely lifestyle also comes to an end. While lionesses generally remain together throughout their lives and help each other, sooner or later a stronger male will come along to banish the previous overlord who is then condemned to the harsh life of a nomad.

The social life of lions is a complex puzzle that researchers have not yet fully pieced together. It can only be hoped that in the centuries to come they can continue to study these magnificent creatures in the wild.

9

A HISTORY

12-13
Lion hunting was a prerogative of the king. Ashurnasirpal (885 - 859 B.C.) is about to stab the beast that has been following his carriage in this bas-relief from his palace of Nimrod, Mesopotamia.

14 top
In 1862, Theodore, Negus of Abyssinia, received travelers surrounded by his four favorite lions.

14 bottom
In Babylon, at the temple of Nebuchadnezzar II (605 - 562 B.C.), the Processional Way was lined by sorrel animals represented on lacquered tiles, among which were several roaring lions.

15
This head in silver, lapis lazuli, and shell, comes from the tomb of Puabi at Ur (present-day Iraq), circa 2650 - 2550 B.C., and is held in the Museum of Archeology and Anthropology at the University of Pennsylvania.

At the end of 1862, Guillaume Lejean, sent by the French government, left the unbearable heat of the lowlands of the port of Massawa on the Red Sea for the cooler Abyssinian highlands. He was bringing gifts from his country in homage to Negus Theodore, the king with an acute sense of theatrics who knew how to surround himself with royal majesty. The monarch always received his guests in his kingdom of Gondar with four lions at his feet, purring like kittens. He was the king of kings, the lion of Abyssinia, and conqueror and domesticator of his totem animals, the kings of the forest and savannahs of Africa. Perhaps without even knowing it, the Abyssinian king epitomized and was glorified by the parade of lions, which had been a regal symbol for millennia. Along with the eagle and the fantastic dragon, preferred symbol of the Far East, the lion had long represented strength, power, domination, and majesty. Its passage from the underbrush to the palace came to pass very early on, together with the earliest urban civilizations. In Nineveh, winged lions with human faces guarded the doors, alongside similarly winged anthropomorphous bulls.

16 top
In a fresco from the tomb of Inherkhau, "Team leader of the Lord of the Two Worlds" who lived during the reign of Ramesses III, two majestic lions protect the rising sun. The tomb is located in the necropolis of the craftsmen of Deir el-Medina.

16 center
This sphinx crushing an enemy, sculpted in the tomb of Khaemhat, has the face of pharaoh Amenhotep III (1382 - 1344 B.C.).

16 bottom left
Nebneryu, the "Lord of Terror" with a lion head, was among the group that greeted the deceased in the kingdom of the dead. Bas-reliefs painted in the tomb of Prince Khaemuaset, son of pharaoh Ramesses III (1186 - 1154 B.C.), in the Valley of Kings.

In Egypt, apart from running with sinuous elegance next to the pharaoh's chariot in war and on hunting expeditions, lions entered the temples and were adored as sacred beasts in the city dedicated to them, Leontopolis, where priests not only fed them, but accompanied their meals with music and singing. Along the avenues, stone statues led to their sanctuaries where they were taken care of and protected, often in guise of sphinxes that married the body of a lion with a human head in an expression of the union between intellectual capacity and physical strength. Moreover, Plutarch and Horapollo wrote that because the Nile River rose when the sun was in the constellation of Leo and therefore the first benefits of the annual flood were seen, the spouts of fountains and water conduits were endowed with good-luck lion faces. This habit spread from the land of Egypt to the rest of the Mediterranean world and explains why today in public fountains in Paris or Milan water still gushes from the jaws of the king of the animals. Cybele, feminine divinity of fertility and the Earth, mother of the gods and men, adored first

16-17
Lion with a human face, the sphinx is among the most famous symbols of pharaonic Egypt. This, in gray granite, discovered at Tanis, comes from the reign of Amenemhat III (1842 - 1794 B.C.)

17 top right
The lion goddess Sekhmet in a gold pendant from the tomb of Psusenne I (1045 - 994 B.C.) in Tanis.

17

18
This efficient representation of a lion in the act of throwing himself on his adversary is painted in the House of the Gold Bracelet, in Pompeii.

19 top
Great hunting expeditions in Africa are recalled by this mosaic discovered in the Villa del Casale in Piazza Armerina, in Sicily. Here a lioness, although wounded, attacks her hunter.

19 bottom left
The Roman emperor Commodus, convinced that he was the reincarnation of Hercules, went into the circus to face beasts wearing a lion skin like his hero.

at Pessinus in Phrygia and then later in Greece and in Rome, where she had a sumptuous temple on the Palatine Hill, was represented seated on a throne with two lions at her side or on a chariot drawn by the same beasts. Yet in *Urbe*, or the Eternal City of Rome, which became the capital of *Orbe*, or the world, lions were not merely sculpted in marble, painted in murals on the walls of patrician houses, or composed in mosaics on the floors, but were alive, vigorous, ferocious, and kept in the cages of circuses from which they exited for the show in order to combat gladiators – in imitation of Hercules who killed the lion of Nemea in one of his twelve labors – or to devour defenseless prisoners condemned to death, such as those first meager Christians to which Nero wanted to attribute the burning of the city. Exhibitions featured not single wild beasts, but whole prides of lions, to the great disbelief and delight of the people: the dictator Sulla dumped about a hundred such beasts into the arena, Pompeii as many as 600 "of which 315 were maned," noted one scrupulous chronicler, and Julius Caesar, 400. In the imperial era, Romans tried to renovate the repertory by making animals fight each other: lions against elephants, bulls, bears, tigers, panthers, and rhinoceroses. Elagabalus, the most whimsical emperor, had the idea of using ferocious animals for chariot races and yoked lions and tigers together. History has not recorded who won. Commodus on the other hand, who fostered such a morbid passion for the games that he claimed his true father had been a vile gladiator instead of the wise Marcus Aurelius, personally descended into the arena 735 times, stabbing elephants with his spear and cutting lions in two with his sword. After many victories he wanted to assume the title of Hercules Romanus, presenting himself with the attributes of a semi-god, a lion-skin, and an enormous club with which he shattered the skull of a few unfortunates disguised as beasts. For this last achievement he claimed to also be the Conqueror of Monsters. So records ancient history, memorializing what is perhaps a notoriously infamous calumny.

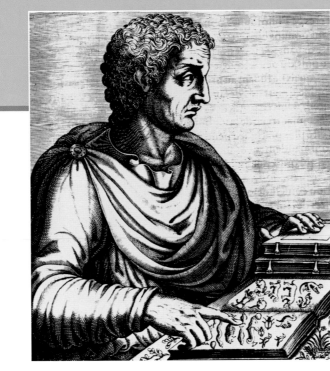

20
A dragon, an elephant, a lion, and a leopard seem to live peacefully in this miniature in a codex of the Naturalis Historia *of Pliny the Elder, completed in Siena around 1460, now in the Victoria & Albert Museum in London.*

21
All that classical antiquity knew or invented about lions is contained in the encyclopedia of Pliny the Elder (23 - 79 B.C.), pictured here in an imaginary portrait from a French engraving from the seventeenth century.

Promoting a labyrinth of true and untrue facts, Pliny the Elder's *Naturalis Historia*, (that vast and admirable encyclopedia of classical antiquity gathered with omnivorous and whimsical erudition) became a sort of bourgeois manual of fantastic zoology. Citing all the believable and unbelievable sources, above all his great predecessor Aristotle who composed a *History of the Animals* for Alexander the Great, Pliny wrote that the lioness was so lustful as to mate willingly with other beasts such as the leopard, and that because the lion was jealous and sharp-eyed and able to recognize adultery by smell, the female would betray her mate only if she were far away, downwind, or able to wash herself quickly in a river. The lioness always gave birth to five cubs the first time, and with every successive pregnancy one less until she finally became sterile with the last litter. They are extremely sober animals: they rarely drink and eat on alternate days, and when they have fed to satisfaction for three days they abstain from food. However, they are also greedy, therefore whatever they eat they swallow whole, save when they must "put their claws in their throat to extract the excess" when they feel too full; and they do the same if they must escape when they are sated. Among ferocious beasts the lion is nonetheless the only one who demonstrates mercy towards those who beg: it spares those who bow down before it, and when it gets angry it loses its temper with men rather than women, and with children "only if it is very hungry." Otherwise, only in old age does it attack man because it no longer has enough strength to hunt other prey. In Northern Africa, it was believed that they could understand the meaning of the prayers. Pliny cites personally gathered statements: a slave of the Djetulai (the internal region of present-day Algeria)

told him that he was attacked by many lions while he was spending the night in a forest and that he convinced them to spare him by begging the strongest of the animals and claiming to be a poor woman refugee of unfortunate health, unworthy of their glory. The encyclopedist gives credit to the story and adds that the nobility of the lion can be seen in its reaction to danger: not only does it despise the hunters' arrows but prefers to fight rather than surrender. And when it is chased, the lion withdraws with disdain, stopping at every step of the way in the fields where it can be seen until it penetrates the forest's vegetation, there launching into a violent run because the screen of the trees hides the shame of flight. If wounded, the lion's great powers of observation allow it to recognize who hit him even among a crowd; but if the man who shot the arrow missed him, it will overtake and throw him to the ground, but not hurt him. However, the lion is terribly afraid of the shriek of carriages and the cock's crow. Pliny concludes his analysis of lions by giving examples of their intelligence and generosity: they allow a wounded paw to be cured or a bone stuck in their throat to be removed and then compensate the helpful man by catching wild game for him and leaving it at his feet, purring all the while like a housecat. The most famous story is that of Androcles, which Pliny ignores but which is referred to in many ancient sources. The tale concerns an African slave who escaped from his owner who treated him badly. Caught and brought to Rome to be torn to pieces in the circus, the punishment for crimes of this nature, the man was seen to gently touch the paws of the lion that should have devoured him as the beast recognized he was the very man who, taking pity on it years before in Africa, had removed a thorn from his paw. This unheard-of scene led the cruel Tiberius to concede the slave his life and freedom.

Parts of the fables of the ancients passed into medieval wild animal tales that further loaded the lion and nearly all other ferocious or domestic animals with symbolic and allegorical significances drawn from the Old and New Testaments. In these texts, of which have survived many splendidly illuminated manuscripts, the lion is attributed three main characteristics. The first is its predilection for mountaintops. On many occasions if it happened to be followed by hunters, as soon as their smell reached its nose the lion would erase its tracks with its tail so that its persecutors would not be able to find it. "So Our Savior (Spiritual Lion of the tribe of Judah, root of Jesse, son of David) first concealed signs of his charity in the heavens until, sent by the Father, descended from the womb of the Virgin to redeem mankind who was lost."

The second characteristic is that the lion seems to keep its eyes open even when sleeping. "In the same way, Our Lord was buried after the cross, and while his body slept, his divine nature watched over him."

The third characteristic deals more specifically with the lioness whose newborns "are born dead and remain so for three days, under her watch, until the third day when the father brings them back to life by breathing on them. So did the Omnipotent, resuscitating Christ on the third day after His death."

In the chapters dedicated to lions, many animal tales included imaginary creatures called "leontofonti." They were beasts of small size which, once captured, are burned. Meat poisoned with their ashes is left at the intersection of paths. "The smallest piece of such food is fatal for the lion, who of course harbors a deep hatred of these creatures, and as soon as it has the chance to kill one, does not tear it to pieces, but shreds it with its claws."

24 top left
A famous lion of Christian hagiography is that cured and welcomed by Saint Jerome, in a painting of Sano di Pietro (1406 - 1481), held in the Louvre.

24 center
Adopted as protector Saint Mark, the Republic of Venice took the winged lion, symbol of the evangelist, as its emblem.

24 top right
This proud lion is situated on the front of the Church of San Benedetto in Norcia.

24-25
On the background of Palazzo Ducale and of the Venetian fleet, this Lion of St. Mark by Carpaccio (c. 1460 - 1526), seems to smile at the prosperity and the glory of the Republic.

25 left
In India also the lion had the job of watching over sanctuaries. This one defends the entrance of the temple of Kandariya Mahadeva in Khajurao, in Madhya Pradesh.

25 right
The very elaborate mane seems to tone down the ferocity of this lion that threatens intruders into Peking's Forbidden City.

An animal so tied to Christian symbology had to associate with the saints. A friendly lion, a close relative of the friend of Androcles, kept Saint Jerome company during the long years he spent in the desert. Other very courteous lions introduced themselves to old and weak Saint Anthony in order to help him dig a tomb for Saint Paul the Hermit just after he had died. But, the most famous lion in Christianity was the winged lion that represented Saint Mark the Evangelist and who, taken as emblem for the Republic of Venice after a few of its sailors surreptitiously fled off with the remains of the saint, carrying them from Alexandria in Egypt to the lagoon of Venice, is still camped on the walls of its palaces in the city and on lands that belonged to the "Serenissima" (the nickname of Venice), from Bergamo to Cattaro, Udine, and Famagusta in distant Cyprus.

The iconographic lion is also widely present in Catholic churches. The first Christians used to paint and sculpt lions to denote strength which they had to prove in order to survive persecution, together with vigilance necessary for the faithful to resist the temptation to sin. Henceforth, the habit of portraying lions on the backs of bishops' thrones or to fashion armrests with lion paws was introduced to signify beastliness in the world defeated by the doctrine of Christ and the pride of the Devil subjugated by the virtue of the cross. As demonstrated, the lion could assume positive as well as negative values. Lions can be found in numerous objects of liturgical use such as candelabra bases needed to sustain Easter candles; and of course door guards outside of churches, both roaring and curled up to support the weight of a column, and to carry out the same responsibility for Christ as they did for the lost gods of Egypt. On the other side of the world, in the vast Chinese Empire, curly lions watched over bridges, dwellings, and tombs of important people with equal severity. Unknown to each other, the East and West were accustomed to rendering justice in the same way, *sedens inter leones*, or sitting between the lions, as ancient maps say: the feudal lord sat between the columns of the portico of the cathedral while the Chinese mandrin rendered justice between jade or bronze lions on either side of his seat.

26-27
Some mapmakers used the lion
as the symbol of Belgium: here
is the "Leo Belgicus" in a map
of Jan van Doetecum, printed
in Amsterdam in 1598.

27 top
Rampant lions are present in
numerous heraldic blazons
such as this one featuring
the coat of arms of the
United Kingdom.

27 bottom
The lion is often repeated as a
decorative feature on many old
maps, above all those that depict
the African continent. Shown
here is a map from 1680.

But medieval lions reigned above all over the very particular multicolored fauna that lived in a world apart, prohibited to common mortals: heraldic blazonry, the new science born at the time, thanks to which the aristocracy distinguished itself from the crowd and affirmed its superiority. It was a rigorous science, with its own rules, typology, classifications, and terminology. In heraldry the lion was almost always *rampant*, or standing on its hind legs, in profile, turned to the right with its tongue hanging out, bent over and round at the end, the tail erect and wagging. But, it could also be in groups if it were sitting, defamed if it were missing its tail, lying down if it had lost heart and had to rest, *dragoné* if it grew a dragon's tail, *langued* if its tongue were a different color, leopard-spotted if it were *guardant passant*, armed if it extended claws of another color, sea-faring if it had a fish tail, *morne* if it lacked teeth or claws, and even boorish when it had sexual organs of a different color.

There were, naturally, knightly Orders dedicated to the lion; the first may have been founded around 1080 by one Enguerrand, Lord of Coucy, in the sweet land of France, favorable to errant knights and their undertakings. Even the lioness had its Order, created in the fourteenth century in the Realm of Naples where a woman governed (or ungoverned, according to some sources), the famous and notorious Queen Giovanna. Her followers wore a golden lioness embroidered on their cloak; more than a symbol of honor, it was the emblem of a political party – and enjoyed a short life.

Beyond coats of arms, lions were frequently featured in maps. From the Sahara down they were distributed throughout Africa, Persia, and Central Asia, and kindly fill in white spaces on maps showing their ferocity as if to excuse the mapmaker's geographical ignorance. *Hic sunt leones* came to mean: these are dangerous places, frequented only by beasts. How could they deserve topography?

27

28 top left
*The two felines in this image
are the work of Ulisse
Aldrovandi and come from
the volume* De Quadrupedibus
solipedibus *in the same
author's Natural History,
published in 1616.*

The passage of the centuries and the expansion of the knowledge of the world put Europeans in contact with unknown animals of other continents, and so zoology began to become strict with regard to heraldry. The cataloging of nature was begun, a job not yet finished as many insects exist which have yet to be indexed. But the inheritance of the past weighs heavily, and even though many of the stories passed down through antiquity have been finally labeled legend, nonetheless even in the eighteenth century, the Age of Enlightenment, the great naturalist Buffon did not dispel all the shadows of ignorance. Typically, in his dissertation on the lion, Buffon (like Pliny 1700 years earlier) gave the animal human feelings and behavior: "*The superior numbers and industry of man betrays the strength of the lion and makes him lose courage; and courage is a quality that, for as much as it is natural, is turned on or off in the animal on the basis of his strength to both good and bad ends. In the vast desert of the Sahara, where two very different races of men seem to have separated, black Africans and Moorish peoples, between Senegal and the borders of Mauritania, uninhabited lands that are above the countries of the Hottentot, and generally in all southern regions of African and Asia, where man has refused to live, lions are still found today in abundance as created by Nature: accustomed to proving their strength to all the animals they encounter, the regularity of their victories makes them intrepid and formidable. They are not afraid at all of the power of man because they do not know it, just as they still laugh at his weapons because they have never experienced them. Injuries bother them but do not scare them, nor are they at all dismayed if they see a large number of men. Often one lone lion in the desert will hurl himself against an entire caravan, and after a furious and futile brawl feel weakened, but not run away and instead continue to fight, withdrawing with his head held high, never turning his back. On the other hand, lions*

28 bottom
This nineteenth century engraving by Dumont portrays the French naturalist Georges Louis Leclerc comte de Buffon (1707 - 1788).

29 top
In the Encyclopédie (1751) of Diderot and d'Alembert, the lion took on a more realistic aspect.

29 bottom
In his dissertation on physiognomy, the Neapolitan scientist Giovan Battista della Porta (1535 - 1615) traced parallels between the appearance of man and the animals. Who else looked like Alexander the Great, if not a lion?

who find shelter on the outskirts of the cities and towns of India and the Barbary States, having encountered man and the force of his weapons and having lost courage, obey his threatening voice and do not dare confront him, throwing themselves onto small animals only, and finally running away from women and children, who beating them with sticks have ruined their plans, making them lose their prey. This change, this pacification of the nature of the lion, proves that they are somewhat susceptible to the world around them and that they are docile enough to be domesticated. It is very sure that the lion if taken young and trained along with domestic animals can easily be accustomed to them and live and even play with them: it is sweet and even physically affectionate with its owner, and if its natural ferocity comes out sometimes, it seldom turns on those who have been kind to it. Since its movements are impetuous and its appetite is ravenous, it would be imprudent to believe that they can be assimilated simply by training; it would be likewise dangerous to make them go long periods without food, or to torment them for no reason; not only does it get angry because of bad manners with which it may be treated, but it will remember and even formulate its revenge, just as it keeps memories of gratitude for good deeds. Many examples could be cited...at least to prove that the anger of the lion is noble, its courage is magnanimous, and it is sensitive of nature. It has been often seen to despise its weak enemies, to not care about insults and to forgive them without returning the offense. Reduced to slavery, lions get annoyed without becoming bitter, rather they give up old habits to obey their master, caressing the hand that feeds them, even sacrificing their life for those, condemned to death, that were thrown before them as prey: and almost as if with such an act of generosity they had sworn their friendship, they continue to offer them the same protection, to live alongside them, to put aside food and let themselves be denied sustenance, suffering hunger rather than deny the original favor done to them.

Dear lions, poor lions! From the conquest of Africa by the White Man until recent decades, the massacre was ongoing. Of course, lion hunting was not invented by Europeans: the indigenous peoples had always practiced it. But they limited themselves to eliminating a few specimens particularly dangerous to their herds and flocks, or to killing the beast – most often a male – in a test of courage, in order to display its mane. Furthermore, the weapons that they had available – arrows and spears – were certainly not suitable to perpetrating massacres on a vast scale such as repeating rifles could and did from the second half of the nineteenth century, decimating the fauna of the Black Continent. And, until the European conquest, even where muzzle-loading firearms were widely diffused as in North Africa, hunting wild animals remained an arduous and complicated business that demanded the participation of entire villages. In North Africa, from Morocco to Tripoli, lions caused much damage: living near human settlements, they left their dens in order to feed on mules, horses, asses, rams, sheep, and camels, penetrating into the middle of the towns during the night. The destruction of woodlands in the Algerian interior pushed the lions continuously further south over the course of the centuries. This destruction resulted more from the need to remove wild beasts who found shelter in the forests than from the need for new cultivatable land. Still, at the middle of the nineteenth century, after twenty years of French occupation, an economist calculated that each year a lion killed livestock worth a total of 6000 francs, and that in average lifetime of 35 years, caused damages costing about 200,000 francs.

The inhabitants used various means to defend themselves. When a village was the particular target of a lion, they dug a big pit at least 10 feet deep and four or five wide, in the middle of the livestock pens. This was hidden by shrubbery that the predator used to jump over at the same point every night, being an animal of habit. Once in the pit, the lion could not get out because of the depth, and remained at the mercy of the captors. They could then take their revenge: the miserable prisoner would be the target of outrage of all kinds, insulted, spat on, hit with rocks and sticks and finally shot. Women, old people, and children became ever more ruthless: they truly wanted to humiliate the king of the forest that had hurt them so much. The meat was distributed to all the village, and every mother made her sons eat a piece of the heart so that they would assimilate the strength and courage of the lion. From the mane they made prized amulets.

Another system of hunting was called *melbeda*, or hide and seek. Near a path usually walked by lions a deep hole was dug, about half feet deep and three or four wide. The hole would be surrounded and covered by tree trunks held in place with heavy rocks. A great boulder acted as the door. In this little fortress the best shots of the village lay in ambush, and from a few small openings shot at the beast on its way to drink or hunt. Sometimes the ambush was staged simply by placing armed men on the branches of the trees surrounding the path.

A third method consisted in organizing truly great battles in which tens and even hundreds of people participated, advancing to flush the animals out of the forest. This was the riskiest system, because the chased and circled lion often attacked his pursuers and clawed someone to shreds before his companions could save him and kill the beast; bullets from old rifles had trouble penetrating the lion's tough skin, and it took many well-aimed shots before an adult specimen could be brought down.

In the extreme south of Africa, the Hottentots hunted in a very curious and even astute way. Hidden on the border of a cliff, they placed a putrefying carcass on the ground so that the smell would attract the lion. As the animal started to consume its meal, the men would move a puppet by means of cords and poles so that it seemed to challenge the lion for its prey. At this point, the men would jump on the lion and throw it into the abyss behind it, and then climb down to finish it off.

30-31
The technique used by the
inhabitants of Bechuanaland to
hunt the lion included the use
of sharpened sticks with a
thick tuft of ostrich feathers,
which served to confuse the
animal. Tablet taken from
Wild Sport of Southern Africa
by W.H. Harris, 1844.

32-33
A group of hunters drinks tea
at base camp during a hunting
battue in Eastern Africa at
the end of the nineteenth
century.

33 top left
A White Hunter of exception:
the President of the United
States of America, Theodore
Roosevelt, photographed in 1910
with a dead lion at his feet.

33 top right
After the hunt, a bit of art: the hunter, explorer, and painter Iacovleff paints the prey that he has just killed.

33 bottom
In 1952, during a visit to Kenya, Princess Elizabeth, soon to become Queen Elizabeth II of Britain, took a picture of a lion for the first time.

According to modern ecological wisdom, the Great White Hunter seems rather a fatuous and nefarious exterminator. As books and then the cinema have recorded, his first paradise was in South Africa. At the beginning of the nineteenth century its savannahs were home to millions of animals: packs of antelopes, zebras, elephants, quagga, ostriches, giraffes, rhinoceroses, gnus, lions, hippopotami, and the ever-present baboons. These apes seemed innocuous but were actually endowed with a fierce solidarity: when one was wounded, all the others would throw themselves at the unwary shooter, tearing him to pieces.

34 top left
Cinematic chills and thrills: Charlie Chaplin in the lion's cage in the film The Circus, 1927.

34 top right
Two heirs of royal lineage: Prince Philippe d'Orléans, pretender to the throne of France, photographed in 1919 with a baby lion in his arms.

In that hunting Eden wandered relentless missionaries armed with Bibles in search of convertible aborigines with which to fill their hunting sack of souls. These were also British followers of cynegetic art anxious to decorate their London sitting rooms with elephant tusks, rhinoceros horns, and stuffed lion heads. The most famous of them was Roualeyn George Gordon Cumming. Second-born son of a Scottish baron, endowed with an extraordinary physical force, an indomitable spirit and incredible health, the robust Highlander, in kilt and shirtsleeves at the head of his caravan, became a legend for aborigines and pioneers, a Victorian Nimrod who inspired ranks of imitators. In 1849, after a series of hits along the river Limpopo, his hunting trophies were so many that he loaded nine carts to transport them to Port Elizabeth, where they were weighed before being brought on board: thirty tons.

METRO-GOLDWYN-MAYER CORPORATION

S·T·U·D·I·O·S
CULVER~CITY
CALIFORNIA

In England, the stories about Cumming made such an impression on the initiates of Diana, goddess of the hunt, that a real migration of hunters left for the woods of Southern Africa; the most famous emulators were Oswell and Baldwin, whose reports called to action other imitators. The worst trouble for the unhappy African fauna happened when blue-blooded guests presented themselves. In 1860 the wild game of Orange had the honor to be in the bulls-eye of Prince Alfred, son of Queen Victoria. It was a truly a lovely hunt: a thousand beaters surrounded an immense area of land in which were blocked 25,000 animals, 6,000 of them were killed; also several natives were trampled and crushed by terrorized herds trying to escape.

After a few decades of such shoot-outs, whole species had disappeared: "Nowadays," wrote a South African in 1890, "our plains are bare and desolate." To sportsmen were added merchants, who beyond elephant-tusk trafficking procured lion skins which were well-loved as carpets, as well as cubs to sell to circuses and zoos, and were proud to be able to exhibit the "king of the animals," albeit saddened and lethargic in a cage.

35 top
The Metro Goldwyn-Mayer
lion has roared on movie
screens throughout the
world, seen here on
the corporation's letterhead.

34-35
The French writer
Colette (1873 - 1954)
is stretched out on
a lion skin in this
photograph dated 1909.

HABITAT AND ANATOMY

HABITAT

36 left
The lion cubs survey the
plain from behind a kopje,
big outcrops of rock of
the Serengeti.

36 right
Males have long canine teeth
(two inches on average).

38
The nomadic males of the
Serengeti follow the migration
of gnus and from July/August
on they start to threaten the
herds of Mara.

39
There is nothing more
magnificent in Africa than
seeing a male lion standing
among the tall grasses –
weighing 395 pounds
or more, about four feet high
at the shoulder, and 10 feet
from nose to tail.

Lions shun dense forests, cultivated land, and highly populated areas. Apart from these, they live in a wide variety of habitats. Despite their preference for the open plains, they seem to adapt to most landscapes from semi-desert areas to mountainous regions up to 14,700 feet above sea level, in their single-minded quest for territory rich in prey and fresh water. Their other habitat requirements include sufficient protection against the sun and a landscape affording good protection for their cubs. As far as possible, lions choose to establish their territories in areas providing excellent hunting opportunities. The type and quantity of green coverage affects the presence of herbivores and therefore has an impact on the predators' choice of habitat.

The lions that have been studied the most intensively live in the Masai-Mara Reserve in southwestern Kenya, 160 miles from the capital, Nairobi. The reserve and the neighboring Serengeti National Park in Tanzania are part of a single ecosystem. Set up in 1950, the reserve was expanded in 1961 and currently covers 583 square miles, although only 250 square miles are totally protected. The remaining area, known as the ranch zone, is used as pasture land by Masai shepherds who set up temporary villages within the reserve. The landscape features wide open plains and well rounded hills.

Hilltops are covered with stones, rocks, acacia thorn bushes, and the odd tree here and there. The mean altitude is about 4,900 - 5,200 feet above sea level, and the temperature is mild. Visitors are often surprised at how chilly the nights can get. The Mara river and its tributary the Talek flow throughout the year, nurturing the wetlands. Several seasonal streams, known locally as *lagas*, often flanked by thick bush, scrub, and trees, cut through the plains. All this contributes to create the perfect setting that makes Masai-Mara one of Kenya's richest wildlife sanctuaries.

Relationships between the species at the reserve are ever-changing. While certain populations thrive, others decline. Because of drought and disease, like the outbreak of bovine plague in 1890 that wiped out 95 percent of the gnus and buffaloes, balances can be drastically upset. The eradication of the bovine plague as well as the increase in food reserves has allowed the gnu population within the Mara/Serengeti ecosystem to grow from about 250,000 in 1950 to 1.5 million in the 1980s.

The appearance and colors of the reserve change with the seasons. At the height of the dry season, the ground is a ravaged brown and the grasses a sickly yellow. The animals are weak. Then come the rains. In "normal" years they are on time: April/May for the heavy rains, mid-October/November for the light rains. The grass seems to become green in no time and the

40
This lioness of Tsavo (Kenya) has climbed a tree to avoid a herd of buffalo, and is trying to locate her companions.

41
Even though they are not as agile as panthers, lionesses easily climb trees and are capable of leaping with great flexibility. Adult males, being much heavier, have more difficulty.

42-43
There are about 100 lions in the Ngorongoro Crater. Because of their isolation, this population has some problems with respect to groups in the neighboring Serengeti.

ground turns into a slushy mud. Few can escape getting stuck in the quagmire in these conditions. The wetlands are once again inaccessible to most. Only elephants, buffaloes, and *defassa* waterbucks can venture with impunity into the wetlands in search of pasture. Above all, life at the Masai-Mara Reserve follows the pace of gnu migration. Starting in June, everyone seems to wait for these herbivores. Gnus migrate following the rains and therefore the dates and routes of migration change from year to year. Seemingly unending parallel columns of animals, some extending for 25 miles without a break, advance towards Masai-Mura from Tanzania, beating deep pathways. In the midst of the advancing hordes, thousands of young gnus born in February in the Serengeti plains stumble through the herd for days on end, in search of their mother, lost somewhere in the crowd. When the columns of animals reach the Mara river, thousands of them drown during the crossing, to the delight of scavengers, monitor lizards, catfish, and crocodiles. At the end of summer, the gnus tread the same route on their way back to the Serengeti.

Masai-Mara is part of the lands of the Masai tribe that lives on the outskirts of the reserve. In times past,

they used to move with their herds, following the seasons and the rains in a migratory fashion, although this is no longer the case today. Wild herbivores compete increasingly for food with their ever-growing herds of cattle and sheep, especially in the north of the reserve.

Masai-Mara is the kingdom of predators. Lions, the easiest to find, are spread out throughout the reserve. According to 1992 census figures, the overall population of adults and cubs amounted to 484, divided into 22 prides, plus 74 nomads, one of the highest lion population densities in Africa. The territories of the resident prides form a large mosaic of all sorts of elements. The pride that has been followed for years was baptized Bila Shaka, and had settled on the east bank of the Mara river, close to the famous Governor's canvas camp and the Musiara wetlands. The pride assiduously frequents the south of the Miti Mbili *laga*, located behind Governor's camp landing strip. A large number of animals are attracted by the evergreen pastureland of the area.

The cats like to relax, perched on a termites' nest, an ideal vantage point from which to keep an eye on the herbivores, especially during the rainy season when the high grass reduces visibility.

44
*The territory of the Intrepid pride in Mara
includes the banks of the Talek River, also the
domain of many leopards.*

45
*This big lion cub drinking is a female,
recognizable by the black spots behind her ears.*

46 and 47
The lions of the park of Lake Nakuru love to
take the track under the big "acacias of yellow
fever" in the early morning and evening.

48-49
Gnus and zebras are the preferred prey of the
Bila Shaka pride. But when the migration moves
on, they have to find other victims.

50
*The rain has just stopped and the male shakes
his mane to remove the drops.*

*51 top and bottom
Even though under the rain showers, the lioness
stays lying in the grass. Normally, they try to
keep water off of their coats.*

52

The color of lions' manes varies a lot, from pale yellow to very dark brown. The males with dark manes will be more sought after by females.

53

The lionesses lying in the grass have been forgotten by the herbivores grazing around them, and they await an opportune moment to hunt.

54

Large numbers of lions have been reintroduced into Nakuru Park in Kenya. From time to time, they patrol the bank of the lake under the eyes of pygmy flamingoes.

55

The weather is cloudy and the heat is not as hot as usual. The pride wanders through the plain at a time when they have usually moved in to sleep in the shade, out of the sun.

56-57
*Around seven to eight years old,
the male is at his maximum
strength. He can expect to live
another few years at the head of
a pride if all goes well.*

ANATOMY

A lion at the height of his glory, rising in the high grasses with his nose to the wind, is a magnificent sight. Its power comes from its average weight of 420 pounds with a height of four feet at the shoulder and a length of 10 feet from the tip of its nose to the tip of its tail. But lions vary in size from region to region. South African lions are larger than their East African counterparts and females are 20 to 50 percent lighter and sleeker than males. Sexual dimorphism is therefore more pronounced than in other felines. The mane is strictly a male attribute and gives lions their majestic aura. It starts growing at the age of two years. It varies greatly in color from light yellow to dark brown, bordering on black. In a five-or six-year-old lion, the mane can be nine inches long. It acts almost like a fencing mask, absorbing paw swipes aimed at the head and neck during fights between rivals. While fur coloring is genetically determined in most mammals, a lion's mane can get darker or paler with age, or lose sections after a wound. Not all males are equal. Only some males develop a long, thick mane. In certain regions such as the Ngorongoro Crater and the Kalahari Desert, black-maned males are not uncommon.

Studies on the impact of the size and color of mane on the social status and reproductive success of lions are currently underway. Mock lions with light or dark, and more or less dense manes are presented to animals in the wild. The males tested are more diffident towards the "toys" with long manes while females seem to be more sexually attracted to dark manes. Researchers are also trying to determine the

58
The lion's face is decorated with short white hairs on the chin, the border of the mouth, and around the eyes.

59
Elma approaches one of her companions in the bushes· where they can shelter themselves from the heat.

60-61
The lion's big eyes vary in color from golden to brown, according to his age and the position of the light. Flies are among the greatest enemies of the feline.

impact of inherited genes and diet on manes. Since most of the young males studied leave the survey area before reaching adulthood, it is particularly difficult to compare the manes of fathers and their offspring. Furthermore, paternity can only be determined with certainty through DNA testing. For all these reasons, most of this research is carried out mainly on animals in captivity.

A lion's head is very large, almost rectangular, ending in a large, rounded muzzle equipped with powerful jaws. The teeth reflect the animal's adaptation to the life of a predator. The lion's powerful canines (2.5 inches long in average in males) are slightly curved and very pointed, equally useful for gripping prey and fighting. The molars are used to grind chunks of meat. A lion's age can be determined by its teeth. The sharp creamy-white canines of young lions gradually become blunt and break with age. As the animal grows older, the canines take on a yellowish color and later become caramel brown. The incisors fall out with age and in very old lions, all the small incisors may be missing. Even very young animals sometimes lose an incisor or two. Another indicator of age is the degree of melanism of the nose, which is pink in cubs but becomes black in old adults. This develops as small black pigmentation spots appear at various points and then gradually expand.

The iris of the eyes varies in color from golden yellow to brown. Paws are massive and powerful, with retractable claws designed to grip prey, and in the case of females and lighter cubs, to climb trees. The tail ends in a tuft of dense black fur that hides a spur-shaped horny growth, up to a half inch in length. By swishing its tail, the lion tries to drive away flies, its worst enemies. Tail movements also express anger and grumpiness.

The sand-colored or tawny coat is rarely uniform. On the belly and the on the inside of paws, the fur is softer, longer, and lighter in color. This is probably a typical camouflage technique: a large object is less visible when the parts in shadow are lightened. Under the nocturnal sky, the lion's coat appears uniformly gray. The area behind the ears is always black, in sharp contrast with the rest of the body. The woolly, light tawny coat of cubs is spotted with blackish-brown rosettes, although these will disappear as the cubs grow older. Lions move noiselessly: the soft pads on their paws allow them to walk without making the slightest sound, albeit leaving them vulnerable to thorns.

62

*The points at the base of four or five rows of
whiskers and the spots just above allow each lion
to be individually recognized and identified.*

63

*Adult females weigh from 70 to 390 pounds.
Their slim, muscular bodies are more adapted
to running than those of the males.*

64

*Champagne is observing a vulture
flying above her.*

65

*The fawn-colored coat of the lioness serves as
camouflage in the tall grasses.*

66
*The lions communicate with different facial
expressions. This one expresses aggressiveness.*

67
*One yawns, the other does not. Yawning
is generally very communicative among the core
members of the pride.*

68 and 69
The male's mane is often compared to a fencing
mask. It is supposed to soften the blows of paws
aimed at the head and neck during fights.

*In 1992, this male became one of the residents
of the Bila Shaka pride. Like many of his age,
his face is marked with many scars.*

*When they can, lions drink every day but they
can go for long periods without water. The feline
tongue is not an very effective tool for drinking,
and the lion spends several minutes lapping the
water.*

*72 and 73
The lion's yawn is often not connected to fatigue.
Yawning signals when he is going to get
up or when he is nervous, and a lion may beat
its tail at the same time.*

74 left
Storms happen even during the dry season in Masai-Mara and leave behind pools of water much appreciated by the lions.

74 right
Small termite nests give the Bila Shaka an excellent site from which to survey the plains.

76
The two brothers form a coalition in which they are equal. They mutually serve the pride.

77
These young nomadic males form a strong association. This union allows them, once they attained full power, to conquer their territory.

11 a.m. The lionesses of the Bila Shaka pride and their older cubs are hidden beneath the bushes. Packed tightly against each other, they are sound asleep. Some lie flat on their sides, their heads and paws lying inert on the ground. Others lie on their backs, a paw extended idly upwards, a very comfortable position when it is hot. Lastly, one of the females sits in the sphinx position, its food-bloated stomach looking enormous. Only one of the lionesses, her chin placed on the tip of one of her paws, raises a sleepy eye towards us. Lions rest for nearly twenty hours a day, in Kenya as elsewhere, earning them their reputation for laziness. As soon as it gets hot, they head for the shade. The pride does not have a fixed resting spot. All the lions spend their day in any shady corner not far from where they were awakened by the onset of dawn; it could be in a thicket, on the bed of a dried-up stream, or under an acacia tree. Over the years, it has been possible to distinguish certain preferences, depending on the season, for certain parts of the laga, an area overgrown with bushes arranged in a circle at the edge of the forest area close to Governor's camp. At Manyara in Tanzania and at Nakuru in Kenya, certain lions rest perched on large trees, perhaps in order to avoid being disturbed by the buffaloes that are particularly numerous in these national parks. The lions in the Masai-Mara Reserve, at any rate, do not seem to have developed this habit. There are six adult lions in the pride at the moment. Four generations live together: the first is comprised of Princess, the oldest, then her daughter Aberlour, and probably two nieces, Elma and Anieska. The third generation includes Champagne and Krishna. There are five cubs, aged about 18 months, two females and three males. Two of the lionesses are not with the group.

Since there are no young cubs to look after, the bonds between the females of the pride are more elastic. Similarly, the two males, Superb and Lieutenant, are rarely with them. This is why we find it very difficult to observe them all together. We have just left the two males. They were about a mile away, lying in the shade of a tree. We found them during the early hours of the morning, in the middle of the plain, calmly basking in the sun to dry the dew off their coats. When it became too hot and the flies grew too persistent, they started whipping the air with irritated swishes of their tails, eyeing the shade of the tree, just 100 feet away. However, it seemed that they could not be bothered to get up but broke into pitiful, long yawns. Finally, Superb, his belly almost dragging on the ground, with Lieutenant in tow, decided to trudge tiredly to the comfort of the shade. In order to see lions as other than just large lazy cats, one must wait for nightfall or the early morning hours. Perhaps it is not right to talk of laziness in their case, but would be better to simply view their habits from a pragmatic standpoint. Why should they expend energy when it is not really necessary for them to do so? They manage their time to suit their needs, waiting until temperatures fall and darkness sets in. And since they are the largest predators in the ecosystems that they inhabit, they have nothing to fear from other animals. The need to be ever-vigilant that keeps many other species constantly alert is simply not part of their make-up. We leave the area to let the pride sleep in peace, returning only in the late afternoon. The lionesses and cubs have just started stirring. One after another they break into long yawns. This reaction is neither a sign of tiredness, nor, as in primates, a way of intimidating rivals.

78-79
*The lions stay still most of
the day in order to avoid the
heat but also to digest
their food.*

80-81
*These young lionesses have fun
with each other. Just arrived at
maturity, they must first live
their adult life in the heart
of their birth pride.*

Surprisingly, lions yawn generally when they are just about to get up or when they are nervous or uneasy. The pride then moves on to the stretching session. Putting its four paws together and keeping its head down, a large cub curves its back upwards. Another prefers raising its hind quarters as high as possible, while lowering its shoulders and stretching its paws forwards, with all its claws extended. One of the young females starts scratching a nearby tree trunk with her claws, soon to be followed by two of her companions, intent on imitating her.

At sunset, the two males start to get going again. They stop abruptly at a bush, getting upon their hind feet to sniff the small branches in an attempt to identify any smells. They then rub their heads and manes against the foliage and turn around, their tails held in rainbow fashion, to mark the bush with a jet of urine. They then go on their way to patrol the pride's territory. Suddenly, Superb stops and stands perfectly still, stretching fully on his paws, raises his head, and roars. Lieutenant immediately follows suit. From very nearby, the ground trembles under foot. The lionesses respond softly. In the distance echo answering roars of the males of other prides.

As there are no longer
young lion cubs in the pride,
this one has split into
several sub-groups and
Elma calls to her missing
companions.

83

The females groom each
other. On the other hand,
they do not groom the males.

LIONS SOCIAL LIFE

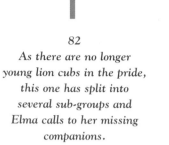

THE PRIDE

Lions are the only felines that live in social groups. Solitary individuals, mostly males, account for about one percent of lion populations. According to a seven-year study on 1500 lions in the Serengeti National Park, the average pride is made up of four to 12 adult females, about a dozen cubs of varying ages, and a single adult male or a coalition of up to seven adult males. Prides with a single adult male are very rare but a pride with a coalition of more than seven adult males has never been documented. The number of cubs varies greatly, depending on births and deaths, and in exceptional circumstances a pride may temporarily accommodate up to 45 members. The type of habitat and the density of the potential prey from season to season have a decisive impact on the size of prides that are generally loosely structured. While pride members may not always be assembled at the same time in the same place, they still belong to the same social unit.

The core of a pride is made up of the females that are generally related by blood: mothers, daughters, sisters, cousins. Lionesses are born into the pride, like their mothers and grandmothers before them, going back several generations. The Serengeti studies recorded a single case of an unrelated female joining the lionesses of a pride, although this is thought to be more frequent in southern Africa. The lionesses of a pride generally live in harmony together for their entire lives, without any sort of hierarchy. The notion of the dominant female is foreign to lions although it is often found amongst other social mammals. This however does not mean that all lionesses do everything in exactly the same way.

The territory belongs to the females, and according to all the studies so far, remains stable for decades. The continuity of prides is therefore maintained by the lionesses. Territories vary in size from between six to 200 square miles. In the Ngorongoro Crater, for instance, territories vary between eight and 150 square miles, while in the Nairobi Park, the average size of territories lies between 10 and 20 square miles. The size of the territory of a pride depends on the type of habitat, the availability of fresh water throughout the year, and the abundance of prey, which must be sufficient to feed the pride all year round, regardless of the season. Certain territories must be huge in order to satisfy all these requirements, and may sometimes overlap with the territories of neighboring prides. In general, the surface area of a pride's territory will not be subjected to equal treatment. Each pride has preferred areas and it is there that the pride will vehemently defend against intruders.

Upon reaching maturity, female cubs will generally remain within their native pride and territory. These young lionesses have no interest in leaving the territory they were brought up in by their mothers during childhood. Here, they are familiar with the best hunting sites during each season, the best places to give birth, etc. Females born into small prides general integrate very well upon reaching maturity, but young lionesses born into large prides have difficulty being accepted, unless the amount of available prey increases sufficiently to feed the extra mouth.

Lionesses leaving the pride generally go on their way

This female has left the pride and has brought with her the older lion cubs. She avoids running into the new resident males which are very aggressive towards the babies and stays in the marshy area.

at the age of four years. They may completely leave their native territory or establish a new pride on the outskirts or a part of the territory of their native pride. This new pride may be a completely independent pride with its own males, or a sub-group of the initial pride of origin, in which case it is not uncommon for females that previously left the pride to return later when they are in heat or new males arrive. When sub-groups are established, they center their activities on different parts of the territory of the initial pride, which they will do their best to avoid. However, should members of the off-shoot pride cross paths with members of the initial pride, the encounter is generally peaceful. Over time, these chance encounters become so rare that the members of the initial and off-shoot prides end up treating each other as strangers.

Upon leaving their native pride, some lionesses travel great distances, to settle down far from the territory of their birth. This type of emigration has not yet been fully studied. In any case, lionesses leaving their native territory take longer to have cubs and have a lower life expectancy than their counterparts who stayed behind. Lionesses leaving their native prides therefore pay a high price for their choice. Besides the size of prides and the scarcity of prey, another reason that can lead a young lioness to leave her native pride is the arrival of a new male. To save their cubs, certain lionesses prefer to flee the newcomer.

Very old females are not generally banished from the pride. They remain full-fledged members up to their death, even if they are no longer capable of bearing cubs or efficiently contributing to the hunt.

The Bila Shaka pride has had a very irregular

history. In 1977, five young lionesses that had just reached maturity left the older females of the pride and set up their own group with three males. These lionesses took over the part of their native territory covering the wetlands which was the pride's traditional hunting ground during the dry season. This sort of behavior was observed several times over the years, with variations that mainly concerned the males. During certain periods, a single coalition of males controlled both the main pride and the sub-group in the wetlands. At other times, the two became independent prides, each with its own males. When Superb and Lieutenant took over in 1996, a group of five lionesses lived in the wetlands without any males. This group, baptized the "Wetland Sisters," was initially made up of three females who avoided all contact with the main pride. In the past couple of years, the Wetland Sisters have given birth to several litters and have recently been joined by two other females, no doubt blood relatives. Lieutenant and Superb control the movements of these females and have most certainly fathered some of their cubs, although they have also killed a few others. Without a well-defined territory and the constant protection of a coalition of males, the Wetland Sisters and their allies find it very difficult to raise their cubs through to maturity.

The adult males of the pride, known as resident males, have no blood relationship with the females. They sometimes come from very far away to take over a pride after chasing away its previous "owners." Fights for control over a pride can be very violent. Sometimes a male will take over a pride left without male protection, either because its resident males died or abandoned their pride in favor of another group.

*The resident males of the
Intrepid pride groom each other.*

Taking over a pride can be a slow process. The new arrivals first settle down at the very outskirts of the territory that has caught their fancy, for several weeks or even longer, before venturing deeper inside on short incursions. One fine day, observers who missed the power struggle or the flight of the previous resident males suddenly found new males at ease with the females at the very heart of the territory, where the old resident males would never have allowed any other male to venture.

Males form coalitions, which seems logical enough given that they have to fight their way into the pride, and a solitary male has little chance of winning. These coalitions last for two and half years on an average, although some have been known to last for up to six years, after which a rival coalition generally comes along and evicts the resident males, just as they themselves had done to the previous residents. This periodic turnover of males helps avoid mating between fathers and daughters. By the time a female reaches maturity at about three or four years of age, a new generation of males would have almost certainly taken over the pride, after having evicted her father and uncles.

In order to better understand the insertion of new male residents within a pride, one must first focus on what happens to young males born into a pride when they reach maturity. At first, male cubs live like their sisters and cousins. The "owners" of the pride tolerate them until the age of about two or three years, after which they must leave.

They either leave of their own accord, feeling the waning tolerance of the resident males and sometimes even of some of the females, or they are chased away by the adult males. In one case, one of the two resident males of a pride was killed by rivals. One of the sons of the surviving males, who had reached the age when he would soon have to leave the pride, fought side by side with his father – assisted by the lionesses – to defend the pride's territory. The rivals were forced into retreat and the coalition formed between father and son lasted several years, with the son living within the pride as a resident adult male. This case is however a rare exception to the general rule.

The young males therefore leave the pride either alone or more often in groups of two or three individuals of the same age. They first remain within their native territory but soon become nomads, seeking out areas where prey is plentiful and hunting together. In lean times, they do not disdain carrion. They live a difficult life, since they are attacked as soon as they enter the territories of prides owned by other adult males. They also have to fight against hyenas who attack them in the hope of stealing their prey. If they left their native prides alone, rather than in groups of brothers or cousins, it is in their interest to set up coalitions with other nomad males.

Even groups that set out from their native pride together often break up and the individuals part ways to forge alliances with other males they meet during their travels. Once they have found the right partners, the young males stay together for several years, covering great distances.

It is routine for all males to spend between one to three years as nomads after their adolescence. At the end of this period, a group of young nomads is physically prepared to take over a pride.

They then settle on the outskirts of the territory of an established pride, looking for signs of weakness or old age in the resident males that they must evict in order to assert their dominance over the pride.

Experts have long believed that coalitions of males were made up almost exclusively by related individuals, that is to say, brothers and/or cousins born within the same native pride. However, DNA testing of lions has recently revealed that nearly 42 percent of all coalitions include males unrelated by blood ties. In fact, two-thirds of all male pairs and half of all male trios (the commonest forms of coalition) are not made up of males sharing family ties. For instance, in the Bila Shaka pride, Lieutenant and Superb are not related by blood, although this is hard to believe observing how they enthusiastically rub against each other and together defend their interests. There is no place for dominance within the coalitions of leonine society. Equality is the rule among males as well as females, unless there is a great difference in age or size, in which case a certain degree of inequality has been observed within coalitions of males.

On the other hand, DNA testing has shown that the members of coalitions made up of more than three males are always related by blood. It would therefore seem that, in seeking coalition partners, lions tend to stick within their original families if their group is larger than a trio.

Other conclusions can be drawn from such research. Overall, larger groups dominate smaller groups and the members of larger coalitions tend to be younger when they first take over a pride. Their dominance is destined to last longer and they will have a larger number of females in their pride. Therefore, it is difficult to understand why solitary males refrain from forging a coalition with a greater number of partners and why pairs and trios (the commonest forms of coalitions) are

not supplanted by groups of four or even five males. They would be able to set up a stronger common front against rivals and maintain their dominance over the females of the pride. The answer to these questions most probably has to do with a sort of genetic self-protection mechanism. The larger the coalition, the greater and more intense is competition between members for access to females, and the lower the probability of mating and transmitting their genes to future generations. Paternity will be dealt with more in detail in the next chapter.

Males and females are assigned very different roles within a pride. Briefly put, lions defend the pride's territory against intruders while lionesses hunt and bring up the cubs. Males get their share of the hunt by forcefully imposing themselves.

The males patrol the entire territory. They move around much more than the females, covering long distances during a single night. Using their sharp vision and acute sense of smell they spy on intruders, seek out females in heat, and locate prey killed by the other members of the pride. They mark the pride's territory with jets of urine or by spraying bushes, clumps of grass, or tree trunks with scents secreted from a gland in their anuses. Lions also mark their territory by urinating on their rear paws while scratching the ground. Glands between the toes secrete a scent that acts as marker on the ground over which lions walk. All these markers create a sort of chemical scent barrier that even a man with a normal sense of smell would be able to detect (from within about 15 feet, apparently). Any lion passing by would certainly get the message. Scent markers last several days and sometimes even weeks, and identify not only the sex, age, and size of the individual that left the scent, but also the time when the scent was left, making for a very handy communication system within a given sector and

reinforcing the bonds between pride members. Females also leave scent markers from which passing males can tell if they are in heat.

Males also assert their proprietary rights by roaring. Roars last between 30 to 40 seconds. Contrary to popular belief, roars are not a sign of hunting, but rather a signal to other male lions in the area that the territory is protected by the resident males of the pride. This "sound marker" has a very wide range and in ideal conditions, over flat terrain and especially when high humidity boosts the sound conductivity of the air, roars can carry for over five miles. While females also roar, their roars are generally much softer and higher in pitch. Pride members recognize each other's roars. Lions roar primarily after dusk and towards dawn, punctuating the night with their "sound markers" at regular intervals. Cubs cannot really roar until two years of age.

These scent markers and roars are in fact rites aimed at avoiding confrontations between the resident males of a pride and intruders. Fights between prides for territory are rare and prides are usually well aware of the limits of their territories, which are scrupulously respected. An intruder surprised in a pride's territory might be immediately attacked by the pride's resident males, but in general, the intruder is chased away by loud roars. The occasional fights with chance intruders rarely end up in serious injuries. Researchers who played back recordings of an intruding male roaring inside the territory of a pride observed an immediate reaction. The pride's resident males instantly set out in search of the intruder daring to roar within their territory. Some of the pride's resident males even attacked a stuffed fake lion placed close to the playback device. Even if a resident male is alone when researchers set off the device, he will immediately seek out the source of the roar, apparently without a thought for his own safety since, in the face of the roars of three potential

challengers, he could very well end up risking his life!

When intruding males do not merely stray into a pride's territory but deliberate invade it so as to evict its resident males, confrontations can be deadly. The pride's resident males put up a united front in such combats, and the fact that they are not all related by blood seems to have no impact whatsoever on their bravery and cooperation. In tests using stuffed animals, researchers have observed that even lions unrelated by blood will fight together as brothers.

The role of lionesses in hunting and bringing up their young will be dealt with in chapters later. Although they are not strictly in charge of defending the pride's territory, they have however been known to chase away intruding males by putting up a united front.

An interesting scene was observed involving the lionesses of the Bila Shaka pride, before the arrival of Lieutenant and Superb. At the time, the pride was without any male protection, the resident lions having abandoned the pride a few months earlier. An intruder had settled above the wetlands several weeks before the incident. One day, he tried to penetrate deep into the heart of the pride's territory. The seven females of the pride at the time had young cubs and were afraid for their survival. They surrounded the intruder. Each time he tried to get away, the lionesses chased him, biting his paws and hindquarters, forcing him to stop and turn to defend his rear. The fight lasted for a long time. The male managed to get away, but was seriously injured. Two of the pride's lionesses were also injured but not as severely as the male. Two days later, the body of the male intruder was discovered, having caused his death wounds.

The lionesses of a pride will defend their favorite hunting grounds, their choice places for giving birth, and their water holes against trespassing females. They follow a more prudent strategy than their male counterparts when confronted with trespassers. When

researchers played back recordings of the roars of intruding lionesses, the females of the pride would come forward to drive them away only when they were greater in number than the trespassers, who were supposed to be at least a pair. Lionesses can count and prefer to maintain a healthy safety margin, since being outnumbered could be fatal. In the Masai-Mara Reserve, for example, a pride with just one or two lionesses would find life difficult, since they would have to avoid all the other prides, and their cubs would rarely reach maturity.

It is quite rare to come across all the members of a large pride at the same time. One could in fact go so far as to say that there are actually two sub-prides, one made up of the males and the other of females. While bonding between males can be very strong, lions tend to be less deeply attached to lionesses. For istance, males will never clean the coats of females. They spend a great deal of their time away from the females and even when they are in the same place, the males somehow manage to stay about 30 feet away from the females.

Bonding between females is very strong and varies depending on their respective affinities. Lionesses can in fact develop a special fondness for some of their female pride members, while others tend to be more solitary in nature. These differences become more marked when there are no young cubs to bring up. When cubs are around, bonding between lionesses intensifies. As a general rule, the smaller the pride, the greater the bonding between its female members. When sleeping together, they will often lie very close, just a couple feet or so away from each other, and it is not uncommon for them to sleep touching one another. Lionesses frequently show outward signs of affection towards each other.

Upon waking and after a hunt, lionesses greet each other. Each bends her head towards the other and rubs her cheek or forehead against her companion's head. This greeting can sometimes turn into a prolonged and complex rubbing of necks and flanks or, on the other hand, can remain symbolical. A lion passing close to a male companion at rest will often simply lower a side of his head to touch the animal as he passes. The latter will either pull its head back or project it forward, anticipating the salutation. Adult males tend to let females take the first step towards mating. Lions rarely take the initiative to greet females, although signs of affection between males are common. When a lion returns to a pride after a time of absence, he is often greeted with a wild show of head rubbings from his companions. The skin above the lion's eyes secretes chemicals that are exchanged when lions rub their heads together. Experts have speculated that these secreted chemicals give off an odor recognizable by all pride members and thus functions as a sort of membership card within the pride. In any case, these greetings are part of the social link between all pride members.

The "greeting" is often followed by body care. The top side of a lion's tongue is covered by forward-curved horned papillae that are used to grip food, remove dust, lick blood, and extirpate parasites before they have time to get a firm hold on the animal. In fact, the tongue not only cleans, but also combs the coat. Lions seem to enjoy licking the faces of their companions, although they rarely lick other parts of the body, save for the females who thoroughly clean their cubs. Social cleaning is more frequent among females. Adult males rarely clean each other, accounting for their dirty tussled manes. In any case, adults keep their own bodies very clean.

As in all communities, relationships among members tend to get more aggressive when an essential element, such as food, becomes scarce.

88
Anieska chews the nape of Aberlour's neck, unaggressively. There are no dominance issues between females of the pride.

89
A lion cub over one year old is seen off by his mother.

90
All the adult females of the pride are on the lookout. A silhouette in the distance troubles them.

91
Four lionesses stare at the buffaloes in front of them.

92
*Lions adapt anywhere as long as they
can find water.*

93
*The females of the pride pass a lot of time
together. They are all related.*

94
The hunt starts with games among the lionesses.
The hunt can wait...

95
The lion cubs chase and try to catch each other
as they would hunt their prey.

It is a pleasure to watch the mother play with her young, a sign of good health. The pride loves these big fallen tree trunks that create a wonderful playground.

98
One of the males of the Bila Shaka pride was
attacked by the females and another male one
day, without apparent reason.
Then, everything went back to normal.

99
A nomadic male was cornered in the bushes by
the resident males. He will manage to escape
but in pitiful condition.

100 and 101
In 1996, the Bila Shaka lionesses united
against a male that was trying to take control
of the pride. He died of his wounds.

102 left
Between two mating sessions, the couple can be tender.

102 right
There is no mating season for lions. The females can be in heat at any period of the year.

104
We find the couple in the early morning very near to where we left them the night before. During coupling, the lions move less.

105
Brown Mane tenderly licks a female in heat with whom he has isolated himself.

We left Mara for a few weeks. On our return, we are told that Superb and Lieutenant were sighted several times in the company of the same female. She must be in heat for the two males to follow her so closely. We decide to trace the three of them. They are quite easy to find since leonine couples do not hide and even when in full heat, do not seek any sort of protection. Generally, the lions do not make any particular effort to be seen either and must be sought out either on the beds of lagas, in the thick of dense shrubs, or in high grasses. Our search methodically focuses around the area where the three lions were last sighted, and it is not long before we find them, since they have not strayed far. We soon find that our previous speculation about the female being in heat was correct. Aberlour lies next to Superb. Lieutenant sits about 150 feet away and seems to cast an envious eye on his companions. As usual, the three lions are totally indifferent to us. This is not always the case however. Once in the Serengeti Natural Park, we were attacked by a male lion who was busy mating with a female when we approached. Our presence made Attila, as we nicknamed him, very aggressive and he mounted a serious charge against our old Land Rover, the top of which had been removed to afford us a better view. Attila's attack took us by surprise and scared us quite a bit. Aberlour gets up and goes to urinate. Superb follows her feverishly and sniffs at her urine several times while breaking into a grimace, with his mouth open, his nostrils pulled back, all his teeth exposed, and his eyes half closed. Then, in a type of foreplay, the male and female rub their heads together and sniff at each other's groins. The female seems ready, but at the last minute moves away and rolls on the ground before getting up and trotting off 200 feet more or less. She then lies down again. Her partner insists and she ends up by presenting him with her hind quarters. Mating can now take place. It lasts just a few seconds. Aberlour lets out a long growl and grimaces as though to threaten an adversary. Silent at first, Superb emits a sort of painful-sounding moan as his pleasure increases, and he bites the nape of his partner's neck. After the mating, Aberlour sends a slap to her companion, with her claws pulled in. He quickly gets away. She then lies down again, a few feet away, and is soon joined by Superb. Ten minutes later, they start moving and mate once again. This is the beginning of the Aberlour's heat and the interval between mating is brief. Throughout the day, Lieutenant keeps his distance, without even attempting to come close to the couple. A few gnus venture to within a few feet of the couple, but are ignored. For the entire week that they spend together, Aberlour and Superb will not hunt and will eat very little, helping themselves once or twice to the food hunted by the other females of the pride. As soon as Aberlour is on the move, Superb is up and follows her every step. This lasts for several days. The only difference is one morning, Lieutenant is no longer to be seen close to the couple. It is only the next day that we find out why: Anieska has also gone into heat and he has started to follow her around. The frequency of the mating between Aberlour and Superb starts tapering off. Both of them seem to have lost weight, and at the rate they go about, they must indeed be famished!

Lionesses in heat have a pronounced sexual behavior and actively go in search of a partner. In general, they choose males from their pride, but if all are out wandering – as often is the case – they may also accept a nomadic male passing through their territory or choose a partner from among the males of neighboring prides. Sometimes they will parade in fronting of roaring lions. Similarly, the males of a pride will mate with all the females in heat that they come across, although they will chase any outside female from the pride's territory if she is not receptive.

Once she has found a male, a lioness in heat moves her tail in the air and rubs against him or lolls at his feet, provoking him. The male follows her feverishly because along her path, she leaves a spray of secretions from her anal glands, mixed with her urine. The lion sniffs this several times and then raises his head in the "Flehmen" posture, pulling in his chops. Any strong smell provokes this reaction. Like many other mammals, lions possess a specialized odor-detecting organ, known as the vomeronasal organ, that allows them to analyze the hormone level of the female and therefore gauge her receptivity. Sometimes, a lioness in heat will attract several males who will follow her around in a state of great excitation. With their manes ruffled, their tails standing up, they will nervously shuffle around her. The strongest of them will intimidate the others who eventually withdraw. There is in fact little rivalry between the males of a pride for a female in heat. Once he has claimed her, a male will not leave his partner's side. If he does, he is often promptly replaced by another, who will have been keeping a close eye on the couple from a few hundred feet away, hoping for just such a windfall. If no replacement is forthcoming, the female will seek out another partner herself. Sometimes, the lioness herself will take the initiative to change partners, having no doubt that the first to impose himself was not really up to the task.

Lionesses do not have mating seasons, but are sexually receptive several times during the year, except during gestation and nursing. Their periods of heat are highly irregular, sometimes following intervals of just two to three weeks but sometimes several months. The frequency of the periods of heat apparently depends on the availability of prey. Periods of heat can last between one day to over one week, although two to five days seems to be the average duration. In a pride, females tend to synchronize their periods of fertility.

While some experts attribute this to an odor that the first lioness in heat secretes as a message to her companions, others speculate that it is the male that produces a specific pheromone to which the females react. As a result, when ten females of a pride all go into heat at the same time, the pride engages in wild mating that can sometimes last weeks on end, during which the exhausted males do little else. This time around, 27 cubs will be born. This sort of synchronization has also been observed in other species, and in certain cases, it has been known to extend to all the females of a population, as in the case of East African gnus: 80 percent of the females above three years of age all give birth during a three week period that starts at the end of January.

Like all felines, including domestic cats, lions are "induction ovulators." This means that the ovule leaves the ovary only after mating. This mechanism is especially adapted to species in which females are solitary. For instance, a female cheetah cannot be absolutely certain that there will be at least one male nearby when she is in estrus. If no mating, and therefore no ovulation, takes place, no great harm is done, since she will soon go into heat again. On the other hand, this type of ovulation is not very logical in the case of lionesses who live in social groups. In principle, the males of the pride are never too far away. This ovulation mechanism in lions is almost certainly a vestige of a period of their evolution when they were a more solitary species.

The lion's penis is covered by pointy granulations. Penetration is painless. However, when the lion withdraws from the female, he provokes in her a sharp pain that is thought to stimulate ovulation. It is at this time that the female, reacting to the pain, becomes aggressive and the male pulls back to avoid the paw stroke that the female generally sends his way. Mating itself lasts just a few seconds but is frequently repeated, about every 20 minutes so long as the female is in heat, an overall average of 50 times in 24 hours. George Schaller has recorded 360 couplings in eight days. Only a species that has nothing to fear from others can afford to devote so much time to sexual activity. What do lions have to be afraid of while they are mating? Even at the end of this very tiring period, they are no more vulnerable than before to other predators.

The sexual endurance of males is really impressive and has no doubt improved over the evolution of the species. Natural selection weighed heavily in favor of stronger and more resistant males. On the other hand, the process seems to be surprisingly inefficient. In fact, despite an average of over 300 couplings during each period of heat, cubs will be conceived during only one out of every four or five periods of heat. This means that a lioness must mate on an average of over 1000 times for conception to take place. While induction ovulators must mate often – since frequent mating increases the opportunity for the reflex mechanism of ovulation to take place – three or four days of intense sexual activity are not necessarily significant in terms of reproduction.

However, this remarkable sexual prowess would seen to almost be in contradiction with the aim of the male to ensure that his genes are passed on to future generations. As the number of couplings increases, a lion's sperm becomes less fertile, and after a certain point, is in fact totally ineffective in conception. Lions therefore mate so frequently for purposes other than reproduction. A male is in fact obliged to perform in order to keep his chosen mate for himself. To be fully sure of his paternity of all a female's offspring, a male must mate with her throughout her in-heat period. Otherwise the lioness will seek out another mate up to the end of her in-heat period. And in this case, the lion runs the risk of inducing ovulation without fertilizing the ovule – since his sperm gradually weakens – creating the possibility for another male to father the lioness's cubs. Therefore, although there is little chance of conception, by mating frequently a lion ensures that other males do not fertilize the female's ovules in his place.

108

The male couples nearly 200 times with his partner over a period of three to five days. Despite this infernal rhythm, chances for conception are weak.

Another consequence of this system is that after several days of intense sexual activity, the male will surely be a lot less fertile for a certain time. Should he come across another female in heat, he has little or no chance of fathering her cubs.

It is natural for males who take over a pride to kill all the young cubs living with the lionesses when they move in. Males reach full physical maturity by about six years of age. It is only at this time of their life that they may hope to be successful in replacing the resident males of a pride. As previously mentioned, the dominance of the resident males over a pride lasts only for about two or three years on average, after which they are generally replaced by younger rivals. One must bear in mind that males rarely live more than twelve years in the wild and generally start declining physically after the age of nine. On the other hand, cubs remain dependent on their mothers for very extended periods of time and the interval between births is generally between 18 months to two years. Males who allow females to bring up cubs born before their arrival would have to wait at least a year to be able to themselves father cubs. This means that they would contribute to protecting and bringing up the offspring of their predecessors, and logically, they would generally be unable to ensure that their own cubs reach maturity before they themselves are replaced by younger and stronger rivals. This would run counter to the interests of their paternity and evolution in general. On the other hand, if all the cubs in the pride are killed, the females would be ready to mate with the new residents just a few weeks later, furthering the new males' goal of reducing the interval

between births. Researchers have calculated that females will conceive again within about four months after new male residents have moved in with the pride.

Such infanticide is not uncommon in the animal kingdom, especially in the case of species where males have access to females for only a limited period of their sexually active lives and where the average interval between births is long. Male hippopotami, for example, also kill the young born to other males before they as newcomers assert their dominance over a group of females.

Periods of transition, when dominance shifts from one coalition of resident males to another, can often totally upset the life of a pride. In general, mothers do not really defend their very young cubs against new resident males, perhaps because it is simply not worth the effort. These newborn cubs are of relatively little value even in the eyes of their mothers – who have invested little time and energy in them – and will be replaced frequently and quite quickly during a lioness' reproductive lifetime that generally lasts for about 11 years. Furthermore, the mortality rate of cubs is very high during the first year of life. Nevertheless, some lionesses with very young cubs will attempt to fight off the new resident males. Since lions are much stronger than lionesses, these mothers are generally destined to lose a one-to-one fight. If several lionesses get together, on the other hand, they sometimes succeed in protecting their young. Lionesses with older or nearly full-grown cubs will sometime flee with them upon the arrival of new males, and will later do their best to avoid all contact with the new residents. They live almost like fugitives on their own territory where

This morning, Black Mane and the female have mated every seven or eight minutes. They then slowed down the frequency of their frolicking.

they are no longer safe and generally not welcome in the territories of neighboring prides. Occasionally, they will join their pride companions when they kill large prey, but without their cubs. Their aim is to try to protect their young until they are old enough to fend for themselves. In certain cases, it may be months and even years before all the females of a pride are once again reunited.

A large number of popular guidebooks on Africa point out that lions kill the cubs fathered by their predecessors in order to ensure that the females go into heat, since, the guides explain, females generally do not go into heat until their cubs are about 18 months old. This explanation seems to be based on pseudo-science and conjecture rather than fact. Domestic cats, for instance, go into heat even while their kittens are not yet weaned, and there is no particular physical reason for lionesses to deviate from other felines in this regard. Researchers in Botswana have analyzed the feces of lionesses to study the link between the presence of reproductive hormones in the feces and the behavior of male lions. They found that when the estrogen level was high, lions often broke into Flehmen grimaces, and concluded that lionesses go into heat before their cubs are weaned. However, these researchers also observed that even without any change in the resident lions of a pride, lionesses rarely conceive until their cubs are grown. Although this seems to be logical, since cubs remain dependent on their mothers for quite a long time, these elements appear to be contradictory. In fact, females certainly show little interest in males, rejecting all sexual advances until their cubs become independent. Despite

this, the lions continue to pursue the females, even if they have little chance of mating, especially if the lionesses are in a group. An isolated female may be forced into mating, but such mating sessions are rather short, rarely lasting more than a day, and ovulation does not take place. Lionesses can therefore go into heat much earlier than was previously thought, although they will not conceive. They are in fact capable of ignoring the messages sent out by their hormones for as long as their cubs are dependent on them.

In light of this new research, infanticide among lions takes on a slightly different connotation, although the end result, to ensure the paternity of the new resident males, remains unchanged. New resident lions kill the cubs fathered by their predecessors, not to force the females of the pride into heat, but to change their behavior and ensure that they are receptive to mating.

Furthermore, observers have often noted that upon the arrival of new males, the females go through a period of intense heat, actively seeking partners everywhere and mating very frequently. Are they trying to test the sexual prowess of their partners and their ability to maintain control over the pride, or are they rather bonding with these new resident males? It may also be that the lionesses are creating an opportunity for coalitions of stronger males to discover the pride and drive out the new arrivals. In any case, the lionesses do not conceive immediately, for reasons that are not altogether clear. It is however quite certain that each mating session does not result in conception, even when the resident males are not replaced. Some researchers speculate that by upsetting the lives of the females and putting them into danger when they

attempt to protect their cubs, the arrival of new males may provoke the release of stress hormones that inhibit the production of the hormones required for ovulation. As a result of this inhibitory effect, the females go into heat normally but do not ovulate.

Some lions father a large number of cubs while others die leaving few or no offspring. Researchers have calculated that a male in a large coalition statistically fathers more cubs than a member of a smaller group of males. But although this calculation is based on an average per individual in the coalition, it does not take actual paternity into account. DNA testing has recently revealed that all the males within a coalition are not equal in this regard. The first male to find a female in heat, jealously keeps watch over her, mating repeatedly. The fact that the lionesses of a pride are often in heat at the same time ensures that paternity is distributed among the males, although at Okavongo for instance, females tend to go into heat at the same time rather rarely. In any case, various studies have shown that in coalitions of three or more lions, paternity is not equally distributed: of the hundreds of lions falling into this category, it is often the same individuals who father most of the cubs in their prides.

So long as the males of the coalition are all related by blood, this phenomenon does not raise any serious problems. All the individuals in the coalition would have an interest in jointly defending the territory of the pride and ensuring the best chances of survival for the cubs of the pride up to maturity. The altruism of the males in defending the young fathered by other lions of the coalition would be rewarded by the fact that the family genes passed on by their brothers or cousins are

protected. But recent research that suggests that even males who are not related by blood will defend the territory of their pride with just as much courage as the others, raises questions regarding the motivation of these males in terms of reproduction. Some of these lions in fact give up all claims to paternity, while at the same time expending effort in protecting and bringing up the cubs of others. While their membership within the coalition ensures them access to the pride and its females, a right they would be unable to acquire on their own, they gain no benefit from this at all in reproductive terms. Equality in paternity among lions is observed only in prides dominated by pair of males. Each one of the pair shares equally in procreation, and therefore even if they are not related by blood, they have every interest in defending all the females and cubs of the pride.

Despite the inequality in procreation between males, coalitions made of three males unrelated by blood are quite common. This seems to belie Darwin's theory of evolution. On the other hand, it could explain why associations between males unrelated by blood are generally limited to three individuals. The benefits, in terms of paternity, would be in fact too unattractive.

It was long thought that the males of a pride fathered all the cubs of the pride's females. This was widely considered as convincing proof that the advantages males stand to gain by taking over a pride far outweighed the risks involved in driving away its resident males.

In Okavango Reserve, researchers have often come across cases of cubs that could not be related to the male residents of their pride. Research into this is still underway.

110
The lovers rest without cares between copulations. For many days, they will neither hunt nor eat.

111
This Bila Shaka couple totally ignores the gazelles who watch them with some anxiety.

112
The lioness is in heat but she has not yet decided to mate. She repels the advances of the male for a moment before presenting him her rump.

113
The end of mating is violent. Black Mane frees himself quickly from the very aggressive female.

Another issue that is unclear is what happens when the females of a pride are already pregnant when a new coalition of males asserts its dominance. The females have miscarriages. Some researchers feel that the lionesses then fake periods of heat so as to mate with the new males. Similar behavior is said to have been observed in primates, where females mislead the males into believing that the young born later are actually theirs, a sort of protection against infanticide. A simpler explanation could be that the production of a high level of estrogen towards the end of pregnancy – a peak detected by the males – could mislead the lions into believing that the females are in heat. Insofar as the females are receptive to mating, the cubs born later would be accepted by the newly arrived males as their own. This explanation that may seem rather simplistic, is quite plausible, since lions cannot count!

Scientists are very much in the dark about the kind of life a nomad lion leads. A great deal of research into this remains to be done. In any case, from time to time, and on a rather irregular basis, these nomads follow nomad or resident females for periods ranging from several days to several weeks, depending on the vigilance of resident males. In this way, they obtain a decent meal by accompanying the females in their hunt.

Similarly, they will mate with all the females in heat that they come across, including females belonging to established prides. They live a rather hard life, since they must often hunt alone and are often attacked by resident males when they venture into the territory of a pride. In general, a male will be a nomad at the very beginning of his adult life and then much later on, after he has been ousted from a pride by rivals. But with a bit of luck – if he has not been totally deserted – he manages to find a new pride.

Old lions end up alone and are forced to hunt for themselves. They vie with hyenas for the remains of the prey left by other predators, getting into ferocious fights in which they are often wounded. In the Masai-Mara Reserve, hunger often leads them to seek easy prey in the *bomas* of the Masai tribesmen, who then kill them.

Despite the difficulties, certain males will remain nomads for their entire lives. Is this really a choice or did they simply lack the opportunity or the strength to become residents? Science has still not found the answers to these and other questions such as whether nomads actually father cubs.

Male nomads are very interesting, from a genetic standpoint. They are often the genetic link between isolated populations and allow genes to circulate, limiting consanguinity in certain populations.

Scientists have long wondered why males do not leave the pride when their cubs are over a year old and are therefore no longer subject to infanticide. The males could well leave the cubs to their mothers and go off in search of other opportunities. In fact, males have been known to abandon their prides in the Serengeti, as well as in the Kruger and Okavango Reserves. These males then father cubs with the females of neighboring prides. Even if they do not abandon their pride, all resident males tend to explore the outskirts of their territory in search of additional females to mate with. These attempts are obviously vigorously resisted by the resident males of the neighboring prides. Some lions somehow manage to dominate two prides at the same time. Regardless of whether they are nomads or residents, all male lions try to expand their sphere of influence.

The male sniffs the urine of the female, his
chops pulled up in a characteristic smirk. Thus
he tests the level of hormones in the urine.

The rain does not calm the passion of the couple.
The female does not hesitate to give the male a
big slap at the end of copulation.

LIONS SEXUALITY

116 and 117
This lioness absolutely does not want to mate and she clearly demonstrates her will to the male.

118
*Black Mane follows the female step by step,
sniffing her smell.*

119
*Black Mane bites the nape of his partner's neck
while copulating, which only lasts a few seconds.
At first silent, towards the end he lets go a sort
of meow.*

120
*Anieskai is no longer in heat. She wants to
rejoin her companions and listens for their calls
to know how to relocate them.*

121
*Due to the frequency of his mating,
the male lion is a symbol of strength and virility
in many African tribes.*

THE FAMILY AND
THE EDUCATION
OF THE YOUNG

122
Three lionesses of Bila Shaka
have left their young alone in
order to hunt. The
synchronization of births in
a pride favors the survival
of the cubs.

124
The young males left their
birth pride, chased out by the
residents. They still prowl the
family territory.

125
The lionesses have on average
two to five cubs, but the
mortality rate in the first
year is very high.

That year, we returned to Mara in July, after an absence of over three months. We found Champagne with three cubs, just five weeks old, and Krishna who had also given birth to two cubs, more or less at the same time. She was resting with them in the bushes. Princess and Elma were with them. Elma's cubs were born that winter and were about six months old at the time. The females spent almost all their time on the banks of the laga. It was the period of the year when the first gnus started arriving from Serengeti, providing the lions with plentiful prey. Migration exerts a decisive impact on the survival of lion cubs since their mothers produce more milk when they themselves are well fed. Superb and Lieutenant were also resting not far from the pride. The youngest cubs suckled while making small cries and pulling avidly on their mother's teat. Fed up with this behavior, Champagne pushed them away and they lay down beside her, pressed against her body. They seemed to be the most recent additions to the pride. Aberlour and Anieska were nowhere to be seen. We spent our days with the pride and left them alone for the night, only to come back to see them again at dawn. The females did not venture very far during the night and came back early in the morning. They were often already back by the time we get to the pride. Elma's cubs, who were nearly weaned, routinely sought out the teats of Champagne or Krishna whose cubs protested with an intensity surprising for their age and tried in vain to defend their rightful place. Both mothers allowed the older cubs to remain at their teats for awhile before driving them away. On the fourth morning, we decided to try to locate the missing females, and set out to patrol the length of the laga, moving towards the wetlands. Suddenly, we came across a female with very large teats, with dark circles around her nipples.

We recognized her as Aberlour. We followed her at a distance and she lead us to the bed of the laga towards a hiding place that we are familiar with since we had spent quite some time at the spot three years ago, when Princess had also hidden her litter in the same spot. The Bila Shaka lionesses rarely sought out places other than this part of their territory to give birth. This area is full of sheltered, peaceful places where they can hide their cubs. We parked our vehicle a short distance away from Aberlour, so as to be able to get a better look. From time to time, we managed to identify four little tawny bundles. Although our line of sight was not excellent, we estimated that they were about three weeks old. Aberlour lay down and allowed them to suckle. When she turned over, we wondered how come her cubs were not crushed under her weight, although they appeared safe and sound on the other side of her body. Another vehicle approached the ditch and its passengers also tried to get a look. But they made too much noise and Aberlour got up and showed her teeth. It was simply not the right time to try to get too close. Unless something unpleasant had happened to her, Anieska also should have been hiding somewhere with her litter, since she mated not long after her companions. She ought to have given birth in the last few weeks. We spent the next few days either at Aberlour's hideaway or close to the remainder of the pride. During the night, Aberlour went hunting, leaving the cubs alone, without protection. She sometimes joined up with her companions to take part in a few ambushes, but otherwise hunted alone, selecting prey from among the gnus in the area. One morning at dawn, we made our way, accompanied by a pack of hyenas running parallel to us. Like us, they too were headed to the cubs' hideaway. Aberlour had not yet returned from her nocturnal hunting raids.

126 and 127
The cub is the only survivor of the litter. In the pride that he is soon going to rejoin, all the other young are much older and his chances for survival are weak.

Although we were not supposed to take any action at all, we feared for the survival of the cubs. The hyenas came very close to the cubs and sniffed the ground all around them. Sooner or later, they were bound to find the cubs. Happily for us, Aberlour rushed quickly up the laga bed and leapt onto the hyenas, dispersing them. She thoroughly licked her cubs, happy to find them safe and sound. This incident obviously led her to change their hiding place, since the next day we found no trace of the cubs at this spot. Some cameramen in the area told us that they had been sighted about a half mile away. The practice of changing hiding places in order to avoid attacks from other predators is common not only in lions but also in hyenas, cheetahs, and leopards. In fact, if the hiding place is not changed frequently, predators will soon be attracted to the spot by the scent of the cubs or by the tracks that will inevitably be formed all around the hideaway.

As the days stretch into weeks, the pride surprisingly remained in the same general area. We generally had no trouble at all locating the lions. Why would they need to move? The cubs were well-protected and prey was plentiful at the moment, with gnus and zebras heading the list. After having "moved house" the last time, Aberlour had hidden her cubs in a part of the laga that was heavily frequented by a herd of buffaloes. We always found the buffaloes around when we got there.

The history of the buffaloes' relations with the lions of the pride was punctuated by ups and downs: sometimes, it is a young sick juvenile who falls victim to Superb, at others, it is an old buffalo killed one night by all the females after stubborn resistance, but on some occasions, like this one, one of the cubs is killed. Aberlour was stretched out on the laga bed when the herd approached. The female, taken by surprise, since she did not hear

them coming, immediately scrambled up a nearby tree, while three of her cubs managed to get under a tree trunk. The fourth did not make it. Caught in the midst of the crowd of hooves, he is thrown high into the air. We saw him fall to the ground motionless. The very confused scene lasted just a few minutes, but left a deep impression on all of us. Champagne's and Krishna's cubs grew quickly and became increasingly playful. They were cute with their spotted coats and large, expressive, and mischievous eyes. One morning, we found Aberlour and her cubs with another of the females of the pride. There were now eight cubs in the pride. In the beginning, Aberlour did not allow the older cubs near her little ones, since they had to first get used to their new environment. Very soon, however, they were perfectly at ease with their companions. All the pride's day-to-day activities were focused around the "nursery," a sort of meeting point at which the cubs could easily assemble. One morning, Aberlour, Champagne, and Krishna decided to parade their eight cubs right before our eyes under the morning sun. Champagne started it by taking one of her cubs between her jaws and moving off southwards. The cub complained. He was big enough and did not want to be carried around like this. But the grass was high and it would have been difficult for him to move on his own over this terrain. Aberlour followed suit with the first of her cubs, and then Krishna did the same in turn. We waited. After about ten minutes, the mothers returned and each picked up another cub. Elma and Princess looked on and remained with the other cubs. The third time, we decided to follow the procession. Finally, the entire pride had changed location and had moved to a new area under several large trees on the banks of the laga. All of them were there. This was rather rare for lionesses. We frequently noticed that mothers forgot one

or two cubs as they could not really count. Just a week before, cameramen filming another pride had also observed this sort of forgetfulness. The mother of three cubs, all about ten weeks old, decided to move them to another area. She invited them to follow her with small, soft roars, followed by louder growls since they were apparently moving far too slowly for her taste. One of the three cubs was soon left way behind, and turned back to find shelter at the starting point, mewing sharp cries in increasing desperation. His mother was quite far away by this time. Upon reaching her destination, she settled down quite happily and went to sleep with her other two cubs. She was too far to hear the cries of her abandoned cub, who finally fell asleep. Later in the afternoon, he started crying once again. The cameraman decided to play back his mother's roars that they had recorded earlier in the day while moving slowly in her general direction. The plan worked. The young cub followed the loudspeaker and was thus reunited with his mother. Mothers have also been known to go off hunting and then spend hours trying to find the spot where they left their cubs. One of the lionesses, Lucia, was not seen again, but to make up for her disappearance, Superb and Lieutenant spent most all the time with the other lionesses and the cubs. This behavior is not widespread among resident males, most of which tend to remain apart and independent from the pride of females.

The cubs often came over to play with the males, jumping on their backs and playing with their tails. These majestic beasts, simply allowed them to do as they pleased, without batting an eye. The cubs were well fed and in full form. They were much more active than the adults during the day, much to our amusement. The young cubs tumbled, bit each other, exchanged swipes of their paws, and licked each other. They climbed onto the backs of the older cubs who shrugged them off to the ground. Quite often one of them lay flat, his nose to the ground, hiding behind a bush or rock. When one of his brothers came towards him, he rushed up to playfully attack the new arrival who taken by surprise fell to the ground, where they continued to frolic. A little farther off, one of the older cubs was fighting ferociously with a clump of grass that he bit, held between his paws, and shook, only to move back, take his stride, and attack it in a single leap. When the females lay down, the cubs came to lick the corners of their mouths and rub against their bodies. When the adults went hunting, they only allowed Elma's older cubs to accompany them, leaving the younger ones behind, generally alone, since it is rather uncommon for one of the lionesses to remain with them to baby-sit. The cubs did not leave the hideout until the adults returned. Aneiska finally returned, bringing two cute bundles with her. The other lionesses welcomed her warmly, with huge licks. This reaction really does bring happy reunions to mind. When, oddly for this period, the lionesses hunted far from the laga, they returned later than usual from their nocturnal sorties. How the cubs rushed towards the returning females, mewing long and plaintively! They were obviously famished. If one of the females returned before the others, all the cubs, both hers and those of the others, rushed towards her teats, all at once. The youngest, Anieska's cubs, could not fight and were soon eliminated from the tussle. The others became a single struggling mass, mewing madly. The lioness couldn't withstand this for long and lay on her belly. She displayed her teeth and tried to escape their bobbing heads, biting teeth, and insistent paws. Some cubs even dug at the ground under their mothers' bodies to get to their teats. Calm was restored only when the other females came back.

128
Upon returning from the hunt, the lioness is welcomed warmly by her young.

129
The cub pulls so hard on the nipple that he topples over backwards. He will be weaned when about six months old.

YOUNG LIONS FROM BIRTH TO ADULTHOOD

Lionesses must generally wait about eighteen months between litters. The period of gestation is relatively brief, varying from 102 to 110 days. In the wild, it is often difficult to distinguish between a pregnant female and a lioness who has just had such a good meal that her mammary glands start swelling with milk. When a lioness is ready to give birth, she will isolate herself in a sheltered area such as a crevice in the rocks, a densely-overgrown den, high grasses, or a dry river bed. Between two and four cubs are born with each litter. These small bundles of woolly fur are born with their eyes closed and weighing about four pounds. Their eyes open after ten to 15 days. Nursing can be a rather rough time since cubs hang on to the teat they have managed to get a hold of and defend their place, although they do not have the right to any particular teat and will change at each feeding. During the first few weeks, their mother will always be alert and very protective towards her litter. She will prudently change their hiding place every three or four days, moving the cubs one by one, holding their shoulders delicately in her mouth. Milk teeth appear after about three weeks when the cubs first start to move about, and by six weeks they are strong enough to walk around their shelter. At about this age, they also get their first taste of solid food by picking at their mother's meal. It is also at about this time that their mother will take them to join the pride. The exact age at which this occurs can vary. Sometimes, when ties between lionesses are very strong, cubs may be brought into the pride a little earlier. During the first few days after they are introduced to the pride, their mothers will not allow the others to get close to them, threatening the other lions by showing her teeth. However after an initial period of adaptation, they partake fully in the life of the adults and cubs within the pride. Since births are often synchronized among the females of a given pride, the cubs will normally enter an environment featuring several litters of cubs of more or less the same age. In order to better bring up their young and protect them from the outside, the mothers of a pride generally form a sort of nursery that becomes the focal point of the pride's life. In this way, lionesses can devote more time to collective hunting. Collective child rearing also increases the chances of survival of the cubs, since they are entitled to feed at the teat of any of the mothers within the pride. Researchers have observed that not only can cubs feed at the teat of any of the pride's mothers, but that orphan cubs will be raised by one of the other mothers. This very permissive attitude is characteristic of the species and has reinforced the image of great cooperation between lionesses.

Recent research into this phenomenon has placed this rather idyllic image into a slightly different context. While lionesses do nurse the litters of their companions, they always try to give priority to their own cubs and routinely reject the advances of other hungry cubs. But lionesses need plenty of sleep, and

cubs quickly realize that in order to feed at the teat of a lioness who is not their mother, it may be better to wait until she is asleep, since she may not then have the strength to resist. Researchers have also realized that a female will be more inclined to nurse the cubs of her close blood relatives (her mother or sisters) than those of other pride females. By analyzing the amount of milk produced by the mother, scientists were surprised to find that it depended on the amount of food eaten by the mother and not the number of cubs in the litter. This explains why mothers with only one remaining cub will be more inclined to nurse other cubs. At the same time, lionesses with a large litter to feed would find it difficult to accommodate other hungry mouths. Therefore, if lionesses do practice collective nursing, it is because they sometimes produce extra milk that they are willing to share with blood relatives. Thus the behavior of lionesses in this regard is not as noble as it may seem.

Spotted hyenas also collectively bring up their young. Mothers often deposit their young together in a hole and watch over them for short periods of time. Each feeds its own young and then goes off to sleep elsewhere. Scientists have observed the hyenas at the hole and noted that each female is solicited by the young of others at least as much as a mother lioness, although a female hyena tends to resist these advances much more energetically.

Cubs are very sociable and will lick their mother all over, much more than she licks them, since adult females seem to prefer to lick their adult companions. They feed solely on milk for the first three months of life, and are then gradually weaned by their mother, although many continue to feed at their mother's teat, depriving their younger kin, until the age of one year or even more. During the early months of their life, meat is more of a plaything than food for them. Young

cubs quickly learn to hold on jealously to a piece of meat and to fight ferociously for a piece of bone. Several cubs will often desperately pull at a piece of meat, each trying to get full control of it, while growling madly. At the same time, they can also die of hunger at just a few hundred feet from their parents, incapable of orienting themselves in the high grass or crying out loud enough to be heard. This is why lionesses avoid leaving their young alone for long periods of time. Cubs grow their adult teeth between nine and twelve months of age. Teething is accompanied by sharp pains and fever that can sometimes even kill a cub.

Cubs grow up pretty fast. Their growth depends especially on the amount of food they get. A well-fed cub at 18 months can be as large as two-and-a-half-year old who has frequently gone hungry. Males grow faster and develop a larger head than females. Cubs do not accompany adults on hunts until they are at least four months old. One or two lionesses may remain with the cubs, though - unlike the African hunting dog and some other species that never leave their young at an unguarded hole - this is not a fixed rule with lions. The dog remaining to watch over the young will be fed by those who went hunting earlier, who upon their return, will regurgitate part of the food they ate at the site of the kill. This does not happen with lions. If female lions bring down a large enough prey, one of them will go back to fetch the cubs and bring them to the site of the kill. However, starting at four months, they will follow the lionesses around everywhere but will not directly take part in hunting, merely following their mothers from a distance. As they observe their mothers at work, they learn the tricks and techniques of hunting. To teach them, females will sometimes beat prey to the ground without killing it, allowing the adolescents to complete the kill. Clumsily at first, they will try to suffocate the herbivore that is generally immobilized, as though paralyzed. Because of their lack of experience, they often let go of their grip, allowing to herbivore to get away. This learning procedure requires several trials. By the age of one year, cubs are generally capable of killing prey and by two years old can hunt on their own. But they still are not fully trained and only adolescents or very large cubs can attempt to bring down a zebra or outwit a gnu that has detected their presence. During their training, cubs will not be able to experiment with all types of game. For instance, in the Okavango Reserve, researchers have identified up to 19 types of prey for certain prides. It is obvious that during their youth cubs will not have the opportunity to learn to hunt them all.

By the age of about two years, differences between females and sub-adult males are already quite marked, reflecting the signs of role-sharing between males and females in leonine society. Young lionesses are much more vigilant, exuding a liveliness and self-assurance that is lacking in their brothers and cousins who are larger but more apathetic. When the pride is on the move, it is often the young females that set the pace, especially when adults seem to lose all eagerness to get ahead. On the other hand, young males indulge in more aggressive games and assert their physical superiority around carcasses. During the period in which adolescents are trained to hunt, they remain on the pride's territory even though they move around independently of other pride members with increasing frequency. Meetings with resident males are still friendly, but not for long. When, at last the time comes for males to leave the territory of their native pride, the resident males will have become very aggressive and even some of the females may encourage the hesitant young adult to leave the pride.

130
When they are young, the cubs manage to climb vertical tree trunks with their sharp little claws.

131
A cub very much appreciates his mother's grooming.

PLAYTIME

Cubs only feel safe enough to play in the midst of the pride. They try their courage against each other and prepare for hunting through harmless games. They also climb on the bodies of resting adults and try to involve them in their games. During the rare lean periods, they are not in the best of health and totally stop all games. Otherwise, playing is part and parcel of their lives. Like elephants or monkeys, lions are particularly playful, although their games are quite different from those of young baboons whose idea of fun includes hanging from another's tail while playing among the branches. However, cubs love playing with the tail of a brother or an adult and rolling in elephant dung. A tortoise is also a great toy. They approach the animal rather fearlessly and beat on it a few times with their paws, naturally causing the tortoise to withdraw completely into its shell. Surprised, they stand back and wait for further reactions. When nothing happens, they try to pick it up in their mouths and this is no easy task. Such play can take on various forms. Feverish races between cubs are fun to watch and when they decide to play with a porcupine, it is not always a good idea. An unusual object such as our vehicle does not frighten them. The larger cubs pull on the rope that we had once attached to the front of our vehicle. On some nights, they shook our vehicle so much that we could not sleep in the overhead tent.

How do lions, elephants, baboons, cheetahs, and other animals perceive play? Even for experts on behavior, defining play is a real headache. In any case, when they play, cubs spend a great deal of energy and also take great risks, since they can sometimes stray away from their mothers without realizing it and predators are never too far away, waiting for just such an occasion. Despite the risks, the benefits and advantages of playing are obvious: by developing his body, a cub develops strength. Playing therefore prepares cubs for what they will have to face throughout their lives. The playfield is a schoolroom where young cubs learn cunningness and improve their skill and creativity. All these qualities will be of great help to them in their adult lives when they will have to conquer a pride or hunt. Playful animals also tend to react better to unexpected events.

The games the cubs play reflect the society in which they live, as they mime the gestures and behavior of their parents. Young lions generally share their little discoveries such as a piece of wood or bone, and if there are any quarrels they also learn to pit their strength against a companion. Older cubs will not normally hurt smaller cubs. The sex of the cubs also influences play and fights between young male cubs are generally more serious.

Play is also important for another reason. Both in animals and in Man, play allows for violent instincts to be channeled. The stronger animals are placed at the same level of the weaker. Adolescent elephants will

February and March 2001 were abnormally rainy – and the mortality rate of the lion cubs born between December and March was nearly 100 percent.

kneel so as to be allow younger elephants to climb over them. Older cubs within a pride will never use all their strength against a weaker companion. That is how they learn to play together. Also, by reducing his own chances of winning, the individual with the upper hand also prolongs the pleasure of the play. When one sees large cubs fighting, standing on their hind legs, one feels that they are engaged in ferocious combat. But at a certain point, one of the adversaries lies down allowing his rival full access to the most vulnerable part of his body. The other combatant obviously does nothing to hurt his companion, because while growing up he has learned to recognize the rituals and rules of social life. Furthermore, during these fights, the attitude of the combatants clearly indicates that these are only fake combats. The mouth is open and distended, the teeth are only half-exposed. These are signs of pleasure and good mood, each showing the other signs of friendship. Both canines and felines add to these signs a specific body language such as a curved back, extended front paws, raised hind quarters, and a strongly wagging tail.

In any case, all animal species do not perceive play in the same way. The less a species has evolved, the less its young needs to learn to reach maturity and therefore the less the species will play. Even among the more evolved species that play the most, play is fully important only if the animals are free from vital concerns such as food and reproduction. When food is scarce, the animals save their energy and the cubs no longer play. One even feels as though they have been suddenly struck by sadness or melancholy. The contrast between this behavior and their liveliness and joy a few weeks later when nature turns to their favor is really quite extraordinary.

Whatever form play may take, scientists are now sure that it is vitally important. Recent research on the brain has revealed that the play could be as important to life – both in animals and humans – as sleeping or dreaming. This was demonstrating by following an inverse reasoning: the absence of play in young animals, as in children, leads to serious pathologies. Studies on the behavior of primates, especially chimpanzees, has shown that animals deprived of play during their youth are immature, introverted, and shy. Both in captivity and in the wild, such animals are unable to adapt socially. Animals born in captivity and raised alone are incapable as adults to communicate properly with others and do not find their place within the social hierarchy, being unable to court and therefore mate with any females.

Play is clearly important and no doubt vital for young animals. It promotes better physical development and facilitates their social skills. But play should not be perceived from such an analytical perspective: it may well be that cubs play simply because they have fun playing. And play is not reserved to the young. Adults also like to play, albeit devoting much less time to this activity.

SURVIVAL RATES FOR CUBS

The mortality rate of lion cubs during the first year of life is very high. When a pride is not very stable and prey is not abundant, the mortality rate increases. Between two-thirds and three-fourths of the cubs survive up to adulthood. These calculated estimates vary from region to region and reflect climatic conditions that can be more or less extreme from year to year. In the Serengeti Reserve, the survival of cubs is closely linked to the rain system. The dry season generally extends from June to October, and during that period the mortality rate in the plains is at its highest. In the rainy season, from November to May, the herbivores come down into the plains, leaving the wooded areas of Seronera. As a result, during very wet years, cubs in this area are the most likely to die of hunger. Furthermore, excessive rainfall during the wet season can have a negative impact on the prides living in the plains: the scarcity of food in the wooded areas, arising from the heavy rains that drive herbivores into the plains, will end up by attracting nomad lions into the plains, creating a danger to cubs who are susceptible to being killed by ambitious nomads. In certain years, all the cubs in the Serengeti Reserve died within the first year of life. The average mortality rate for the last 20 years has been 57 percent (compared to 35 percent in the Ngorongoro Crater).

In any case, a large number of cubs fall prey to hyenas, jackals, leopards, or are even killed by other lions that do not belong to their pride, who find them without protection. It is rare for these lions to eat the cubs they kill. Cubs can also be decimated by disease and hunger. They often die of hunger as a result of the social structure of their species that does not seem to be designed to manage the problem of extended periods during which prey is scarce, small, or difficult to capture. As we have seen, when a pride surrounds a carcass the males eat first. The cubs are the lowest in the pecking order, as it were. Sometimes males, who ferociously keep females away from the carcass, will invite the cubs to eat with them. This makes genetic sense for these males since the cubs bear their genes while the females are not related to them by blood. But when prey is scarce, cubs often go without food, so much so that should this continue for an extended period of time, cubs can die of hunger. In lean times, as a result of a lack of vitamins as well as parasite attacks, cubs lose nearly all of their fur and become gradually weaker as they experience increasing difficulty in gaining access to carcasses. Even though the adults may be losing weight too, they are much fitter than the cubs. Luckily, cubs do not die very easily. They can recover their coat, their playfulness, and their health with surprising speed if food again becomes plentiful.

The phenomenon of infanticide upon the arrival of new males in a pride accounts for 27 percent of cub mortality. Quite apart from infanticide by males, the researcher Judith Rudnai has observed that a lioness may of its own accord abandon the last surviving cub of its litter if all the other cubs of the litter die very young. This would allow her to save her time and energy in order to conceive a new litter as soon as possible, with better chances of survival. Another important factor that contributes to cub mortality is the negligence of lionesses, belying the phrase "like a lioness defending her young" as a simile for the virtues of maternal protection.

In fact, lionesses are rather bad mothers, at least according to our value system. In fact, newborns are left without defense, alone in a hideaway when their mothers go off hunting. Then, even when the young are in groups, lionesses do not always make sure that they are watched over. Many lionesses abandon cubs when they change hideaways, and later when moving about with her cubs, a lioness may forget to wait for the ones last in line.

The survival rate of cubs varies greatly depending on whether the mother is a nomad or lives in a pride. Whereas during a good year a pride female can manage to ensure that close to half her young survive beyond one year of age, nomads generally lose close to 90 percent of their cubs during the first year of life. In the first place, a nomadic female gives birth to fewer cubs than a pride female, and secondly, these cubs are vulnerable to attacks by hyenas or adult male lions. Even if they manage to escape predators, their mother will have a tough time feeding them when they reach a meat-eating age. In fact, hyenas or male lions steal the prey of nomadic females who have to leave their prey unattended while they go off to bring their cubs to the feast. Nomadic lionesses therefore tend to produce very few surviving offspring.

Within prides, litters that are born in synchrony with others survive better than litters raised out of synchrony. This is because, even if lionesses are not as community-minded as was once thought, nursing and cub-raising are best done collectively, since this allows a cub to feed even when the mother is not present. Furthermore, cubs raised collectively run a much smaller risk of being left without protection while their mother is out hunting. On the other hand, young cubs have a lower chance of survival within a pride if the pride includes lions that are older than the newborns by several months. In fact, these older cubs will have precedence over their younger brothers at table, and if there is even the slightest lack of food, the younger cubs could be forced to starve to death. A lioness' best chance is to give birth at the same time as her companions.

138
*This cub is playing with a weaverbird's nest fallen
from an acacia tree.*

139
*At four weeks, a cub lets out little cries. Cubs are
not able to really roar until they are two years old.*

140
*An older lion cub contains his strength when
he plays with a younger one.*

141 top
*Two lionesses of the Keekorok pride have returned
from the hunt. All the cubs, even those that do
not belong to them, hurry to nurse.*

141 bottom
*The lioness is irritated by the cubs that pull
too hard on her nipples. She frees herself
and shows her teeth.*

142 and 143
*At first, the lioness calmly put up with the
games of her cubs. Then she had had enough
and showed them her irritation before getting up
and settling down a bit farther away.*

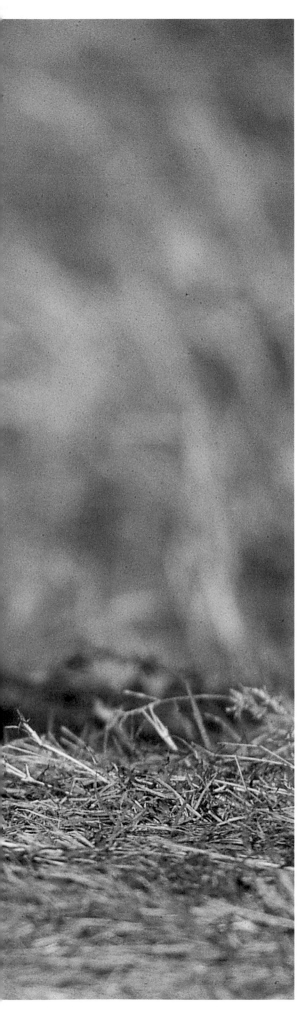

144
At a very young age cubs begin to play. They hide in ambush among the rocks or in the bushes and then continue playing.

145 top
The termite nests are much appreciated by lion cubs as well as adults.

145 bottom
These cubs' woolly coats are light fawn, spotted with brown-black rosettes. Their fur takes on a uniform color with age.

146
As this cub demonstrates, getting licked may require an acrobatic position!

147
When the lionesses are lying down together, the cubs always try to get a few free cuddles.

148
A cub gnaws on twigs when teething.

149 top
Playing is not a privilege limited to cubs;
adult females also play among themselves.

149 bottom
Like adults, cubs give a characteristic smirk –
head lifted, chops pulled back – when they smell
a strong odor.

150 top
The cubs keep on licking their mothers until
they return the favor.

150 bottom
The cubs, too young to participate in the hunt,
watch the death scene taking place just before
them.

151
Playing can almost cease at the end of the dry
season, when nourishment is rare.

152 top
Everything is a pretext for playing, particularly
small branches or even dry elephant dung.

152 bottom
This two-month-old cub grooms herself
thoroughly. A cub's tongue is strong and rough;
it combs through the fur until it is clean.

153
This very young cub discovers the outside
world. He plays with a stump, with his claws
fully extended.

154
*Aberlour carries her cubs one by one
in her mouth, supporting them with her paw.*

155 top
*The young grow up very quickly. Their growth
depends above all on the quantity of nourishment
they receive.*

155 bottom
*The lioness leads her very young cub to the prey
she and her companions have killed on the
savannah.*

156
*This young male cub bites his sister's nape – a
behavior he will demonstrate later on in mating.*

157
*The cubs stay quiet in the bushes with their
mothers. They want to be forgotten by the
herbivores grazing a bit farther off on the plain.*

158
*The cub leaps onto his mother's rump – as he
will do later on when hunting herbivores.*

159
*In the cool hours of the early morning, the
games are even more intense.*

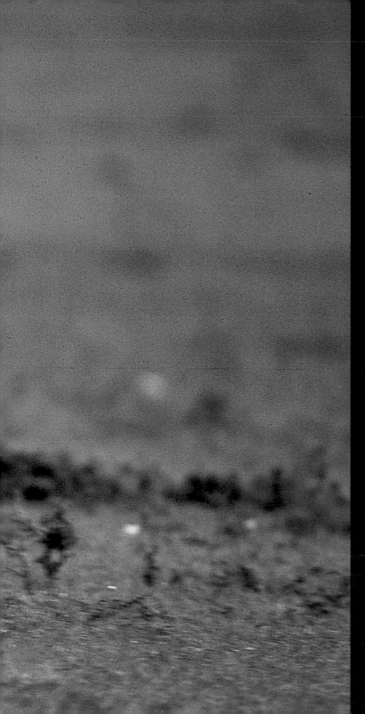

160 top
The cubs try to stay with their mother, who wants them out of the way so she can relax.

160 bottom
The education of the young of the pride is collective.

161
When five or six weeks old, cubs are able to travel with their mother, but the route is long and difficult for them. And the lioness won't wait for them anymore!

162
Two-month-old cubs play in the
rose-colored early morning.

163
While the females sleep near them in the
bushes, the cubs start to wake up. They are
more active at dawn than in the daytime.

164
At birth the baby cub weighs about 4.5 pounds
while the mother weighs nearly 330 pounds.

165
The mothers regularly change their cubs'
hiding place so that they cannot be found
by hyenas, leopards, or cheetahs. But being
crushed by buffalo herds is a risk.

166
*The adolescent is trained to hunt with a
mongoose with which he plays.*

167
*The turtle is an interesting toy for
the cubs.*

166

168 and 169 top
The first time that cubs of five or six weeks have been brought a carcass and tasted meat. They have just been integrated into the pride.

169 bottom
A zebra hoof is more a toy than real nourishment for this two-month-old cub.

170
After heavy rains, cubs must manage on the flooded ground. Excessive rains raise the mortality rate among the very young.

171
After having eaten, the lioness drinks. Her very young lion cub drinks very little; the milk he nurses on is sufficient.

172
*The males spend a lot of time with
the pride when the
cubs are little.*

173
*The males tolerate the young cubs' games
even if they are less patient with them than the
females are.*

IN THE YOUNG

THE EDUCATION OF

173

THE FAMILY AND

174 and 175
*When they have had enough, the males stop the
playing with a growl or a threatening grimace,
exposing their fangs.*

176
*The difference in size between two-month-old
cubs and the adult male is impressive.*

177
*It is not the lion cub that provokes the male's
grimace but the smell left by
a lioness who had been lying with the cub
a few moments earlier.*

ON THE ART OF EATING

178 left
*This newborn gnu of the
Serengeti (Tanzania) was
separated from his mother
during the stampede of his
herd. He stayed glued to a
patch of acacia trees, mistaking
them for his mother. The lion
only had to serve himself.*

178 right
*Superb is devouring a gnu
carcass that he seized from
some hyenas.*

180
*The males of a pride
kill each other as well
as gnus or other
herbivores.*

181
*The lioness is suffocating
a topi. A physical reflex
has plunged
it into a sort of coma.*

On that afternoon, we were going through the sector of the Wetland lionesses, headed towards the territory of the Bila Shaka pride where we intended to spend the night. On the way, we came across a giraffe standing out charmingly against the cloudy sky. As we photographed her, we noticed that she was trembling. We soon discovered why: two small feet jutting out of her rear portion told us she was giving birth! Suddenly the head of the new born appeared and then the entire body slipped towards the ground, propelled by its own weight. During the six-foot drop, the amniotic sac broke open and the umbilical cord snapped. The newborn lay on the ground, and for the first few minutes, did not even have the strength to lift up his neck. His mother licked his entire body, stimulating his muscles. Nevertheless, it was close to an hour before he managed to stand up on his own very long legs. He then pressed against his mother's forelegs to reach her udder. In the meantime darkness fell, since the little giraffe was born late in the evening. The Wetland lionesses must have already left for the hunt. We soon saw two of them breaking onto the scene. The mother giraffe put herself between the cats and her newborn. She used her forelegs to stamp resoundingly against the ground. The lionesses made several attempts to get to the newborn, but were held at bay by the giraffe's hooves. Finally one of the lionesses managed to get a paw swipe at the newborn who fell to the ground and could not get up. This happened after over an hour, during which his mother defended him steadfastly, until she suddenly lost all interest in the newborn and even went off several feet away to eat. The two lionesses were now free to help themselves. It was too late to reach the Bila Shaka pride and we decided to head back to the camp. We caught up with the pride the next day at about three in the afternoon at the resting place the lionesses had selected in the morning. We dozed for about two hours in our vehicle, enjoying a full view of the lionesses lying on the grass. They were certainly far better off than us, in the shade of the bushes! When the heat dropped off decisively, we started being more attentive. The cubs became restless and started playing, much to our amusement. A herd of topi pass by at a reasonable distance, always keeping the lionesses' bushes in their sights. One of the lionesses opens an eye and glances at the passing herbivores. The hunt is on, we thought, but it was not to be, as she slumped back down with a deep sigh. Only the older cubs stopped their games to watch the passing topi. Although the pride did not take any large prey since the previous day, we were now quite sure that they would not be hunting this afternoon. Suddenly, the lionesses started stretching. They got up and greeted each other, then turned their attention to their cubs. Lastly, they cleaned themselves up a bit. They then left the shade of the bushes and took a look around. We had seen no sign of the males since the morning. The light fell brusquely, and the sun was setting over the savannah. It was time to get moving. Aberlour lead the way. The lionesses went in the opposite direction of the herds of gnus that we could see in the distance.

182
The little giraffe was born around 5:00 pm. The prowling lionesses found it after night fell. Its mother defended it for a long time, beating with its front hooves. But the lionesses won!

This was not the first time that we were surprised by the pride's choice of direction. Did they really make a deliberate choice in choosing their path or did they just go off at random, following the mood of the one in the lead? We did not really know the answer to this question. We followed the pride through a large expanse totally devoid of other animals. We had to be very careful since high grasslands can be treacherous and we had to keep a look out for warthog burrows. Towards 8 p.m. the pride stopped to rest for few minutes before continuing on its way. Suddenly the lionesses stood stock still to listen to roars coming from the west. The roars were from the two males of the pride and the females answered them sweetly as they continued on their way towards the Wetlands. Suddenly, there was a sharp change in their behavior. They detected something that we could not yet see (we were driving practically without lights, only using our headlights from time to time). The lionesses detected a group of impalas, a male with his harem of females. They immediately fled in all directions in a panic. The male remained as a sort of rearguard and was the last to flee, when Anieska was almost already upon him. In a final burst of energy, the impala managed to get away from his assailant. The lionesses took no prey this time. One must bear in mind that although they came across these herbivores quite suddenly, the scent of the lionesses was carried by the wind, warning the impalas. Also, they did not actually prepare an ambush. Far from ideal hunting conditions! The pride reunited. The lionesses rubbed heads together and growled softly. This ritual was probably aimed at ensuring that none of the pride lionesses was hurt or rather had managed to get a piece of the prey. And then they were off once again, in single file.

At about 10 p.m., we came across vague silhouettes. A small herd of zebras was grazing peacefully and had not yet detected the arrival of the lionesses who this time were well placed, their scent carried away from the zebras by the wind. Two of lionesses broke the formation, one going off to the left, the other to the right. As they often do during the night, the lionesses proceeded without hiding themselves. The moonlight was very dim at the moment and they ran little risk of discovery. The remainder of the pride carried on directly towards the herd of zebras. The lionesses at the head of the pride rushed forward at random towards the herbivores, causing them to flee in panic. This maneuver seemed to be aimed at distinguishing the weakest of the zebras. And it worked: a young zebra, followed by its mother, fled slower than the others and without knowing it rushed off towards Anieska, who had left the pride earlier to move towards the right. The mother managed to get away from the cat, but her foal did not have a chance. Anieska threw the young zebra down into the grass and held it by the neck to suffocate the animal. One of her companions was already on the scene, and attacked the hindquarters of the animal. The mother zebra tried to get close, but it was already too late. The other members of the pride quickly came together around the small carcass. But they had no time to partake of the spoils, for the two males were already on the scene, eager to enjoy the lion's share. The pair were happily enjoying their meal when Aberlour, frustrated, approached them. Superb flattened back his ears, opened his jaws and pulled back his chops. At the same time, he growled, reinforcing his message: if Aberlour came any closer, he would attack her. The lioness persisted and received a stroke of his paw. In the end, she dropped her efforts and went to wait with her companions, several feet away.

The laughing cry of hyenas could be heard in the distance. The lions were not at all worried by this, since they were protected by their number. Once they had their fill, the two males allowed the cubs to approach the

carcass. But there was little left to eat. Although there was nothing left for the females, they did not seem to protest too much. Prey was plentiful during this period of migration and the females were well aware that they would soon find something else with which to satisfy their hunger. The lions and lionesses then went off to drink from a nearby laga, before lying down to rest awhile.

Later in the night, the pride started off once again. The lionesses and cubs ran around and played with great pleasure, jumping on each other's backs and tussling in the grass. Then they calmed down and things started getting serious. As the crow flies, we were not far from where we had set off earlier in the evening. In the relative silence of the night, the sharp "gnu-gnu" of the gnus in the nearby migrating herds could be heard. The lionesses were now on the alert. Aberlour, once again took charge of operations. She seemed to be at the forefront of the hunt, killing prey, much more often than the others. The females panned out in an arc. They took advantage of the element of surprise, since the grass is high in the wetlands, hiding them from sight. Aberlour leapt into the heart of the herd that immediately dispersed. Three lionesses almost simultaneously killed two juvenile gnus and one adult. It was a good night. The whole pride moved towards the three carcasses. On some mornings we had noted up to eight carcasses, some of which were nearly intact, such was the abundance of prey during the migration season. After the meal, the entire pride, including the males, dropped off to sleep until the morning. As they rested, the hyenas moved in to finish off the remains of the first hunt of the night. This was just one of many almost identical nights in the life of the Bila Shaka tribe, when prey is plentiful. But on how many other nights does the pride go hungry when gnus and zebras are rare, and when the wetlands are so flooded that only buffaloes and cobi may venture into them?

THE LION'S MENU AND HUNTING TECHNIQUES

Lions are obviously carnivores and hunt a wide range of species, even if they do have preferences. Their size and power allows them to capture animals as large as buffaloes and giraffes. In East Africa, gnus are at the top of the list of preferred prey (in the Serengeti Reserve, gnus account for more or less half of all prey), followed by zebras. Giraffes and juvenile hippopotami are much lower on the list. Lions have been known to hunt rhinoceroses, but since this species has become so rare, it is very difficult indeed for a pride to come across one of them. Lions also have the habit of eating grass, especially after a particularly filling meal.

The above list however classifies preferred prey only during periods of abundance. For this reason, small animals were not included. Nevertheless, we have come across lionesses expending a great deal of energy in capturing rather tiny juvenile warthogs, even when the Ngorongoro Crater seemed to teem with gnus and zebras. When prey is hard to come by, when lions have no real choice, everything is fair game. At such times, the menu will include small prey that lions would not normally look at such as tortoises and pythons. Even fruit and ostrich eggs that are quite difficult for lions to break have been found acceptable. The list of preferred prey depends on the lions' habitat and their staple diet is not uniform. They adapt their dietary habits in keeping with the food opportunities available, and some populations have developed rather interesting local specialty tastes. Lions at the Virunga Park in Zaïre regularly hunt hippopotami, while it is not uncommon for prides at Chobe Park in Zimbabwe, and even in Malawi, to hunt elephants, especially juveniles, a habit that is unheard of in East Africa. In the Rufiji River basin in Tanzania, crocodiles are often on the menu. The opportunism of lions allows them to survive even in desert areas, where they feed off the most unusual prey. The "Skeleton Coast" Park in Namibia, a desert area par excellence, lions have been known to feed on dolphins and whales washed onto the beach, and over the years have become quite skilled at hunting seals. They surprise seals as they sleep on the beach and even pursue them into the water, engaging in furious battles. At the edge of the Kalahari Desert, porcupines are often on the lions' menu and sometimes account for one-fourth of their diet. It is true that on such a diet they tend to be leaner than their counterparts in Tanzania or Kenya who would disdain such meager prey. Furthermore, they may be totally ignorant of how to go about it. We once saw a particularly famished Serengeti pride cornering a porcupine just before it could reach its den. The cornered porcupine started clicking its spines and spitting. The lioness leading the hunt was not very impressed and forced the animal on its back so that she could get to its belly, which is not protected by spines. The porcupine somehow managed to get back on its feet and turned the spines on its back towards the lioness who did not hesitate to go at him in any case. Was this the first time she was reduced to pursuing such prey? In any case, the next day we found the pride resting on the rocks. The rash lioness still had a large number of spines in her chest and was licking at all the wounds on her paws. She paid a high price for that meager meal.

188
The female observes her surroundings. She looks out for the possible arrival of males who could take her meal away.

In most cases, three of four species account for 75 percent of the diet of a given population. Towards Seronera in the Serengeti Reserve, these species are the zebra, the gnu, and the gazelle. In Manyara, the zebra, the impala, and buffalo are preferred, and at Kafue in Zambia, the buffalo, the sassaby, the warthog, and the zebra. As a result of the strictly seasonal presence of various migratory species, in Okavango eight species are known to provide 75 percent of the diet of the local lion population.

In the case of certain species of herbivores, the males are relatively more susceptible to attack by lions than the females. One of the reasons for this is that the males of these species are often weakened by fights among themselves for possession of the females on their territory – this happens with gnus for instance – and in the course of their fights and courtship, lose all sense of prudence. Another reason is that the male is often the last to flee, remaining behind to defend his harem after raising the alarm, as in the case of impalas.

While lions are prevalently predators, they are not beneath feeding on carrion. The distinction between prey and carrion is not very clear. Generally, prey is a living animal that is killed by the predator while carrion is an animal that is already dead. But does the lion become a carrion-eater when he eats a buffalo on the verge of death from disease or when he steals an impala freshly killed by a leopard? In any case, lions do not feed solely on animals that they have killed themselves. They have been known to steal prey killed by other predators, especially hyenas, as well as to feed off animals killed by disease or other natural causes. Vultures are often the first to get wind of an animal carcass. When a vulture pinpoints a dead animal, it will make a bee-line for the prey. Other vultures will soon follow suit. Both lions and hyenas keep an eye out for

vultures as they home in on carrion, and the quick-moving hyenas are often on the scene before the cats.

The habit of sometimes feeding on carrion is widespread, regardless of the geographical location of the lion population. All the lions do it, nomads tending to do it more often than sedentary pride residents. Researchers have calculated that carrion accounts for just below one-seventh of lions' total food intake. Feeding on carrion can be dangerous for them, for it is easy to become poisoned by the state of decomposition of the carcass. Cheetahs, for instance, will not run this risk, since they feed solely on prey that they themselves have killed. Lions hunt wherever there is prey. Their territories do not include specific "hunting grounds." The odds are more likely to be in their favor if the terrain features thick overgrowth and an ambush can be easily set up near a waterhole or in an area close to a waterway which can be forded. However, potential prey will not tend to spend too much time near these hazardous areas, and lions are often forced to hunt in areas less favorable to them. In these cases, the success of the hunt depends on their knowledge of the territory.

While hunting techniques vary depending on whether the cat is hunting alone or in a group, there are certain fixed rules. Lions tend to hunt at night, making full use of their night vision capabilities and their highly developed senses of hearing and smell. In terms of pure speed, they run fast, between 30 and 37 miles per hour, but nearly all their prey can run faster, and can maintain their peak speed over long distances, while lions are not long-distance runners and can maintain their top speed for no more than 200 yards or so. When running at top speed, the slightest sudden change in the prey's direction can cause the lion to slip on wet grass or mud. Although lions are super-predators, placed high on the food chain, it is not always easy for them to capture prey.

*Lionesses greatly enjoy baby
warthogs and spend a lot of
energy catching them.*

While lions' efficiency has evolved and increased over the course of time, their potential prey has also improved their escape and defense mechanisms. Since lions tend to hunt animals living in herds, it is easier for the prey to detect the danger. They avoid overgrown areas and are very careful when they are vulnerable – such as the giraffe – and when they are close to water. Zebras, gnus, gazelles and other antelopes can graze just a few hundred feet from a pride of resting lions, in full view. So long as they are in perfect health and remain fully alert, they do not feel that the presence of the cats is a potential danger. They do not feel compelled to flee or even to leave the area.

Lions have better night vision than man because behind the retina their eyes feature a reflecting layer that allows light stimuli to be recorded twice. Their eyes are therefore more sensitive in very weak light. Unfortunately for them, herbivores also enjoy better night vision than man and their eyes also feature the reflecting mechanism. There must therefore be some other explanation for why lions hunt better at night. It may be because of a series of factors. At night, visibility is low, shadows are deeper, the unevenness of the ground can be used to full effect to hide predators, and movements are less visible. However, lions cannot afford to hunt only at night since some animals such as gazelles, for example, go to drink at their waterholes, where they are most vulnerable, only during the day. Other animals, such as warthogs, never venture out of their burrows at night.

To capture prey, a solitary lion must be able to get sufficiently close to an animal without being seen to then suddenly break into a fast sprint and leap at the animal, bring it to the ground, and take by the neck while using all his weight to keep the animal down.

About 100 feet seems to be an optimal distance for the attack to be successful. Lions must be very careful when leaping onto prey since a strong animal could seriously wound, or even kill, a solitary lion. Oryxes, for instance, are very dangerous with their saber-sharp horns, while zebras and giraffes defend themselves using their hooves. Buffaloes can also make good use of their horns. In order to get close enough to the potential prey, lions make full use of all the advantages provided by the terrain, including tree trunks, stream beds, high grass, and bushes. Most hooved animals have excellent vision covering a wide angle. But they are color-blind and their sight is probably not very precise in the case of unmoving objects. Therefore, for camouflage purposes the lion does not need a coat that is perfectly matched to the color of the ground. All he needs is a coat is not too dark or too light. In fact, it is movement that betrays the presence of lions, especially in the open savannah. This applies to both the day and the night.

When the terrain is lacking good hiding places, lions must move furtively while the intended prey is distracted. He therefore moves when the prey is grazing and stops skillfully when the animal raises its head at regular intervals to keep an eye on its surroundings. He then moves forward again, without being seen, as the prey continues grazing. But even then, the herbivore will always keep a watchful eye over its companions, careful to note any change in their behavior and ready to flee at the slightest suspect noise or unexpected movement. This is why most attempts at hunting by solitary males are fruitless. Researchers have calculated that a solitary lion has only an eight percent chance of killing fleeing prey. In the case of a group attack, the success rate rises to 30 percent. When the prey is taken by surprise, the lion

has a 60 percent chance of success. These figures clearly show, as if any proof were required, that the elements of surprise and cooperation between lions are very effective in improving results. Solitary hunting is generally imposed on males during the periods when they live as nomads. But contrary to popular belief, females also often hunt alone.

Lionesses do between 80 to 90 percent of the hunting within a pride. Males, heavier and more easily detected, take little part in hunting even though they are fully capable of taking even large prey such as a zebra or a buffalo. George Schaller estimates that 75 percent of the food eaten by a male lion is hunted by a female, 12 percent is stolen from other carnivores, while the male himself will have hunted but a meager 13 percent. These figures do not apply to nomadic males who cannot rely on females and are therefore forced to hunt much more frequently.

How do a pride's lionesses hunt? According to popular myth, lions are supposed to hunt as in a ballet, with a highly complex choreography. At dusk or at dawn, all together, united with a common purpose, they are supposed to surround their unsuspecting prey and like commando killers, silently open their throats. Various accounts by explorers and hunters have contributed to this myth. They often describe hunts featuring an astonishing degree of cooperation among females, while males deliberately go upwind in order to be detected, causing the intended prey to flee towards the females waiting in ambush. These stories do not satisfy modern-day observers who have never documented males acting in this way. They either directly take part in the hunt or they ruin it by roaring while the females are mounting an ambush, or by sniffing at a female's hindquarters to check on the state of her heat just when she is about to launch an attack.

When they have decided to hunt together, two or three lionesses of the pride will hide close to a herd, while the others will spread out in a semi-circle to attack from several sides at once, driving the panicked animals towards their hidden female companions. Sometimes the inverse scenario is used, with the lionesses encroaching silently upon a herd of herbivores from the sides, as their companions mount a frontal attack on the herd. The final result of both these attack techniques is the same.

Females can choose between advancing towards the herbivores that they covet, or simply waiting until the prey comes closer on its own. Sometimes they will combine both techniques, using the quick raid and the ambush. Lionesses can be very patient. The Wetland lionesses, for instance, are quite used to waiting for hours hidden in the grass close to a waterhole frequented by zebras and gnus at midday. In fact, most herbivores do not drink at dawn or dusk, preferring the hot afternoon hours when lions are supposed to be resting. However, not all ambushes or raids succeed. Overall, only a quarter or a fifth of all hunts are successful. Herds of prey often simply move away from the lions without ever having detected their presence. Moreover, should a herbivore detect a movement or a scent, he will immediately rush to safety. As soon as he is at a safe distance, at least a few hundred feet from the lions, he will then issue a warning call without taking his eyes off his would-be assailants.

It has long been thought that lions live in prides to benefit from the advantages of collective hunting. Research at the Serengeti Reserve has shown that lionesses form hunting groups when they attack difficult prey such as zebras or buffaloes (which can weigh up to 1,100 pounds) or even giraffes. If the cats did not hunt together like this, such prey would remain

unused as a food source. Average-sized antelopes –
such as gnus for example – are in any case put to full
use as a food source, since they are also hunted by
other predators such as cheetahs and leopards. Access
to large prey is the first justification of collective
hunting and the main reason for associations between
females.

In the case of smaller prey – such as a gnu or a
gazelle – hunting is often solitary. But if all average-
sized prey is accessible to solitary cats, collective
hunting can also improve the success rate since, in the
confusion of the initial attack, the fleeing herbivore
often runs within the reach of lions that he has not
seen and that are waiting in ambush.

The females of a pride do not always hunt together
and are in fact quite individualistic. When a female
sets out on a hunt, her companions may or may not
join her. They are caught between the desire to join
her in order to increase the chances of success of the
hunt, and their reluctance to do so because of the
energy required, the stress, and the risk of being
injured that the hunt entails. In any case, if the hunt is
successful without them and the prey is large enough,
they will also get their share of the food. The
advantages of collective hunting are therefore not
always obvious. If a female can succeed alone, it may
not be worth it for the others to participate. This
applies all the more in areas where average-sized prey
is plentiful. The same phenomenon is observed in
other social species including birds, insects, and
mammals. Cooperation is much greater when solitary
hunters require help. On the other hand, it is quite
clear that in lion populations at Masai-Mara and at
Serengeti, cooperation among females increases when
some of the lionesses of a pride have young cubs to
feed. The mothers of these cubs are more willing to

take part in collective hunts.

The success rate of hunts also depends on the
species hunted, falling to 14 percent in the case of topi
and rising to 38 percent in the case of zebras and
gnus. Warthogs are very difficult to capture because
their eyes are placed very high on their heads. While
they eat, with their snouts to the ground, they may
seem totally engrossed in what they are doing but they
are also keeping an eye on their surroundings, looking
out for any sign of threat. At the slightest indication of
danger, they put their paws over their necks and hide
in their holes. Some lions will not hesitate to spend
hours digging in an attempt to reach the animals.

Prides sometimes specialize in a type of hunt that
they become particularly skillful at successfully
bringing off. This technique is used especially when
hunting zebras and buffaloes. In the case of the latter,
the lions prefer to remain hidden and target the slower
animals towards the back of the fleeing herd. They try
to sow panic and isolate solitary individuals. These
hunts are very long and require a great deal of
perseverance, especially since the herd often comes to
the defense of a wounded animal or a herd member
who is cornered, and it can sometimes take a pride of
lions several hours to kill a buffalo. Certain prides like
hunting baboons that they catch at waterholes. On the
other hand, lions are rarely capable of hunting
elephants and of attacking large herds of females and
young, although this has been known to happen in
Botswana. In this case, the attack is open and direct, as
with buffaloes. The attacked herd panics and disperses
in disorder. It is at this point that juvenile elephants
can stray away from the herd or be trampled by
panicking adults, becoming easy prey to the lions who
now only need to keep the adults at bay during the
kill. It has been speculated that these unusual hunting

190
*A male can consume more
than 100 pounds of meat
in a single meal and then
be able to go without food
for a whole week.*

191
*These two males bitterly fight
over the prey that they have
killed, each wanting to take it
in an opposite direction.*

techniques may be transmitted genetically.

A large number of factors contribute to a successful hunt. First and foremost, the direction the pride takes at the outset is important, and lionesses often make rather surprising choices such as going off the opposite direction to a herd of herbivores. The direction of the wind plays an important role although these large cats seem to be totally oblivious of this fact, often failing in their attempts because the scent of the lionesses is quickly picked up by the potential prey. Once they are sufficiently close to their prey, the lionesses must stop to see whether the prey will be detect their presence or continue to move unwittingly towards the waiting cats. Lastly, they will have to react in quick response to what the animals do when the lionesses launch their attack and also see whether there are some weak or vulnerable animals in the herd.

Finally, a successful hunt is far more probable when the prey makes mistakes or when one of the potential prey is handicapped by age - either too young or too old - or is unfit because of an injury or disease. Environmental conditions also play a role: in southern Africa, lions are more inclined to attack giraffes or juvenile elephants during periods of drought whereas they would not bother with such prey during the wet season.

Predatory behavior is part of natural selection as it destroys a high proportion of handicapped or less well-adapted animals. The old as the young are frequently victims of this process, since they are slower in their reactions and flight. But it would not be accurate to say that lions always seek out the weakest of the herbivores, because they also attack a large number of animals that are in perfect physical condition. Nothing could in fact be simpler than devouring a newborn Thomson gazelle or impala left alone by its mother in the grass. These females cannot take their newborns to the herd as they

must first consume the placenta and afterbirth, then clean their young carefully and take it away from the place of birth so as to cover all traces of any lingering scents that might betray the hideaway. The female will later return at regular intervals to nurse her young.

Lions often hold their prey by the muzzle until the prey suffocates. This is known as the "kiss of death." Prey held by a lion to the ground in this way or by the neck dies in a few minutes by strangulation, suffocation, or loss of blood. Smaller animals are killed faster by a bite on the neck. A herbivore is generally not yet dead when the lionesses open its belly. There seems to be some sort of physical mechanism that throws the attacked animal into a sort of coma, explaining why, even if they are not injured, they do not struggle against the cat. A zoologist who wanted to cut off a piece of the lion's prey for himself was surprised to see the apparently dead gnu take flight as soon as the cats were driven away. Lions first devour the muzzle of the victim and then remove its viscera, starting with the intestines. The stomach is often taken several feet away, and a little later one of the lions will cover it with materials such as dirt, grass, and pieces of wood. Lions do not generally play with their prey as a domestic cat might do with a mouse, but this has been known to happen with baby gnus and baby warthogs.

During a single "meal" a hungry lioness can eat up to 65 pounds of meat over several hours, enough to survive on for four or five days. A male can put away 100 pounds, equivalent to about 20 percent of his body weight. To consume an analogous amount, an average person would need to eat 45 large steaks one after the other. When the lions have a large meal, the results are visible: their bellies are swollen and taut. But they do not eat everyday. Researchers have calculated that an adult kills an average of 20 large animals per year.

192
The topi calmly watches the advancing lionesses. He knows they have no chance of catching him in the open.

193
The lioness carries the carcass of the zebra towards cubs that remained hidden while the troupe left to hunt.

194-195
The cubs are healthy, they eat well because the gnus are currently very numerous in the territory.

192

Lions have no table manners at all. Small and big fights can break out between individuals who just a few minutes before seemed on very friendly terms. Rivalry is much greater among hungry animals than among well-fed cats, and disputes are more likely to arise over large prey than over some small tidbit. Thus, when a pride of well-fed lions takes a large animal, all the pride members partake of the feast at the same time, even if they growl, threaten, or hit each other with their paws while continuing to eat. This ends up in a lot of noise and nipped ears for some of the pride members, but no serious injuries are sustained. More importantly, all will have eaten. Being the first to hold a piece of food gives an individual temporary supremacy over his companions. When a lion has finished his piece and comes close to another who is still eating, the latter will growl against the potential usurper and may even attack him. When two lions get their paws on small prey such as a gazelle at the same time, they will often fight between themselves to assert sole ownership of the animal. These fights generally end when the cats, each pulling at the prey, manage to rip the carcass into two or more pieces. This can take some time, since each of the combatants tries to hold the carcass against the ground with his muzzle and paws or by lying on it.

In general, the larger lions have precedence over the younger ones, and males dominate females. Therefore, when they have just captured prey, lionesses will try to swallow as much of the meat as possible before the arrival of their masters, who will make no allowance whatsoever for them. While showing their teeth and claws, they growl, send out jabs with their paws, and keep the lionesses at bay as they eat at their leisure. Their ears flat against their heads, their chops open showing their impressive teeth, the lionesses retreat, abandoning their prey. On occasion, a group of lionesses may get together to recover a carcass from a male. In turn, however, the lionesses dominate the cubs. Therefore, within a pride, if males are present, they eat first, followed by the females and lastly the cubs, starting with the oldest. The young are always the last in line, not because they only get to the prey after the lionesses have had their fill, but also because they are weaker than the adults, who steal everything they can get away with. Females take advantage of cubs exactly as males take advantage of females. The law here is truly survival of the fittest. Fights over prey only become violent during lean times. When prey is plentiful, males will sometimes allow the cubs to eat with them, before the females. If large prey is taken all these quarrels are set aside, since in any case there will be sufficient food left for the cubs even after all the adults have had their fill. It is rather rare for prey to be lacking in areas currently inhabited by lion populations.

A nomadic lion will frequently allow another nomad to share his prey. On the other hand, no member of a pride will allow a nomad or the member of another pride to share his meal.

All the lions in the observed regions drank at least once a day as they roamed through their territories. During the rains, water is plentiful. Streams, waterholes, and puddles among rocks are well supplied. During the dry season, water is scarce, but some could always be found in stagnant pools left in large river beds or in springs. In certain areas, lions have been known to travel several days at a time without water, but in the Serengeti/Masai-Mara ecosystem, they do not need to. They lap water just like domestic cats, a process which is in fact very slow. While lions do not bathe, they can swim very well.

RELATIONSHIPS WITH OTHER PREDATORS

When we first started routinely frequenting the Masai-Mara around 1989, hyena populations were much larger. We were quite surprised at the time by the relationship between these two species. We had just reached the sector known as "Leopard Gorge" when we heard the yapping of a large number of hyenas. Following these cries, we found six or seven lions helping themselves to a freshly killed buffalo, surrounded by about fifteen hyenas. A herd of buffaloes looked on from much further away. We thought that the cats had killed the buffalo and that the hyenas,ß had rushed to the scene. Before our eyes, the hyenas tried to organize an attack by kicking up a real racket. The lionesses reacted violently and resisted. One of the hyenas was left moaning, another bleeding from his hind quarters, and the last in the pack was clearly limping. Several times, the hyenas tried in vain to gain control over the buffalo carcass. Vultures waited in the surrounding trees. When we got to the scene we noticed another vehicle, and after about an hour we approached to say hello. What the driver of the vehicle told us placed the entire scene in a new light. He had been observing a rather ferocious fight between two buffaloes at the edge of the herd. After some time, their horns got interlocked and they were unable to separate. A pack of passing hyenas quickly grasped the problem, and immediately attacked the two buffaloes that could not defend themselves. The rest of the herd tried to provide assistance, but in the ensuing struggle one of the two buffaloes fell. In a desperate effort, the other buffalo managed to extricate himself and flee but it was too late for the first. Two hyenas had already opened its belly while it was still alive, and the others immediately came in for the kill. The hyenas had called out to other companions and attracted the attention of a pride of lions nearby. The hyenas were outnumbered, and so the lionesses, with the help of one of the males of the pride, successfully obtained control of the prize. So our first impression was quite wrong: the thieves were not the hyenas as we had first believed! Scenes like this are quite common and are part of the reason why hyenas have long been labeled as carrion-eaters. Research by Hans Kruuk has gone a long way to change this idea demonstrating that in certain areas hyenas are actually predators, in some cases killing close to 90 percent of the mammals included in their diet. Hyenas hunt in packs, often during the night, relying on their speed and stamina. Frequently, when they are just about to start their meal, lions appear on the scene. Hearing their yapping and cascading laughs, the lions rush to the scene and deprive the hyenas of their feast. When researchers play back recordings of hyena cries to lions, the lions immediately set off in the direction of the sound. Once driven away from their rightful spoils, the hyenas have little choice but to wait for the lions to finish. Since this often happens at night, far from the prying eyes of observers who find the hyenas at the carcasses the next morning, the hyenas are branded as carrion-eaters.

196
*The number of hyenas seems
to be growing in Masai-
Mara lately, after an
important drop.*

197
*Antagonism between hyenas
and lions never ends.
When hyenas do not
have the upper hand,
they flee.*

However, it is equally probable for the situation to be inverted. A lion hunting on his own could easily have his prey stolen by a pack of determined hyenas. Since hyenas generally move in packs, if they are greater in number they can not only defend their own prey, but also steal the spoils rightfully earned by others.

Animosity between lions and hyenas is rather intense, depending on location and especially the density of hyena populations. In certain areas in Botswana, competition between the two species has reached tremendous levels. National Geographic cameramen Derek and Beverly Joubert have written that "only a dead hyena would share its den with a lion." They report very violent fights between the two animal communities. At the same time, in December 1999 AFP reported that hyenas fleeing ferocious battles between their pack and a group of lions in Ethiopia had later devoured a mother and child in the eastern part of the country. When the hostilities ended, after a full half-day of ferocious fighting, 30 hyenas and two lions lay dead. In early April of the same year, similar outbreaks of violence resulted in the deaths of six lions and 35 hyenas in the Gobele Desert, again in the eastern party of the country. Locals spoke of "ferocious violence," "a horrible massacre." They said they had seen a lion fighting against six hyenas, and then being replaced by a companion after he himself was too wounded to carry on. In both the above cases, the territory remained under the control of the lions. What is the reason behind these fights? It could be mixture of territorial conflicts, revenge, the result of a long drought, or even any combination of the above. These two species are old hereditary enemies. The history of their parallel evolution can also provide some explanation. Some researchers speculate that when saber-toothed felines walked the earth, hyenas were huge and sociable. The two species had clear-cut, distinct roles. The cats were large predators who killed very large prey using their huge teeth which, while very efficient in hunting, were rather clumsy and even an impediment to eating, getting caught in the flesh and bones of the carcass. As a result, prehistoric cats left large amounts of food on their prey, probably over 50 percent. In such a scenario, there was plenty remaining for hyenas after the cats had finished. But evolution went forward. Saber-toothed species became extinct, paving the way for species with small teeth, perhaps because, in the end, these species were more efficient. At the same time, the large species of hyena also became extinct. The surviving feline species ate a much greater proportion of the flesh of its prey, leaving much less for the hyenas. As a result, fights erupted between the species over animal carcasses. Thus the hyenas also started hunting for themselves, practically poaching in the lions' territory. In order to put up a better front against the lions, hyenas started forming increasingly larger packs. Since then, the two species fight over the same prey, or more often, the same carcasses. Although lions may kill hyenas, they will not eat them.

RELATIONSHIPS WITH CHEETAHS AND LEOPARDS

One morning several months ago, we found the two males of the Bila Shaka pride on the bank of the laga, lying under two high trees with rather thin trunks. The females were a few feet away with their cubs, who were very young at the time. The scene was made quite comic by the presence of a young leopard who had seemingly just reached adulthood, perched in the branches of one of the trees. The young leopard did not find the situation at all amusing and did not dare leave the tree, since each of his attempts to do so were met by threatening gestures and a show of teeth by the lions. The previous night, when the adults went off to hunt, they had left the cubs hidden in a nearby ditch. Because the cubs were very quiet, the leopard did not detect their presence. As a result, he either chose one of the two nearby trees to spend the night in, or quickly sought refuge in its branches when he heard the adult lions approaching. For whatever reason the leopard ended up in the tree, the lions on the ground had no intention of leaving. It was a question of asserting property rights. They kept a close watch on the cornered leopard for three days, the adults taking turns to remain close by at night to keep watch on the tree. The leopard became very hungry and started moaning. Alerted by its cries, park rangers decided to take action to diffuse the deadlock. Using vehicles, they managed to drive the lions a short distance away from the tree so that their vehicles came between the trees and the large cats. The leopard did not hesitate an instant, and immediately leapt off

into the bushes. It was basically his lack of experience that led to this situation, which is normally quite rare.

Lions (like hyenas) procure a portion of their food by stealing the prey hunted by smaller predators such as leopards or cheetahs. The latter live mainly in large open plains and feed prevalently on gazelles or other small prey that lions would generally disdain. Since cheetahs hunt during the day, conflicts over food between them and lions or leopards are minimal. Nevertheless, they eat very quickly, always alert for any signs of danger, since lions, male baboons, or hyenas routinely attack them while they eat in order to steal their prey. Leopards, on the other hand, prefer terrain offering plenty of coverage and hiding places. This species has a varied diet and does not generally compete with lions for food. Nonetheless they still take their prey up a tree to keep their food safe from the envious mouths of lions and hyenas. Therefore, even if each feline species features its own preferred prey and habitat, lions seem unable to tolerate the presence of any other species on the territory of their pride. Competition is not limited to food raids. Lions have been known to send other cats into flight and to even kill adult cheetahs and leopards, if they get the chance.

Lions – quite like hyenas – will kill leopard and cheetah cubs if they come across any young left untended, although lions will rarely eat such cubs, merely lacerating their carcasses before abandoning the scene. Leopards and cheetahs will also kill any lion cubs left untended.

198-199
Aberlour waited in ambush and surprised this female cheetah who was had to escape as fast as she could. Lions kill cheetahs, mostly the young ones, but they do not eat them.

200-201
The male is absorbed by his meal. The king of the beasts has nothing to fear! He can take as much time as he wants.

202 and 203
The lioness has isolated herself because she is soon going to give birth. An opportunist, she prefers to attack a baby antelope, such an easy prey! And she does not have to share with her companions.

204
Many of the pride's lionesses were waiting in
ambush but only Aberlour "worked." The others
were happy to watch – and then share the
huntress's meal, a very frequent outcome.

205
As nearly always happens in the hunts,
Aberlour puts a topi to death by suffocation.

206
A lioness attains 40 miles per hour at full speed.
In fact, this is slower than many of her prey.

207 top
In Ngorongoro, the lioness lay in ambush near
the river since early morning, waiting for
the zebras that come to drink an hour or two
before noon.

207 bottom
The lioness, at the end of the chase,
synchronizes her gait with that of her victim.

207

208 top
Anieska is in a position to attack; she has cornered a young gazelle behind a termite's nest.

208 bottom and 209
Just after giving birth, gazelles consume the placenta and then leave their babies in the grass, returning to nurse them many times a day for three weeks. Anieska has no problem catching this young and defenseless antelope.

210 and 211
The lion prides of Mara almost never hunt elephants, and cohabitation between the two species is generally peaceful. Nothing prevents an adolescent or adult elephant who feels like playing from charging the felines.

212
This male is going to spend many hours trying to
make a warthog come out of the burrow
where he has taken refuge.

213
The lion has cornered a sick buffalo in the herd.
The mother buffalo will manage to defend herself for
several hours before abandoning herself to the feline.

214
*Until the last moment the male impala tried to
protect his harem – and became
a victim of his duty.*

215
*The two male lions of the pride share this
meal "stolen" from their females without
too much violence.*

216
Lions frequently lick the skin of the animals that they are eating.

217
Lions do not hesitate to stick their heads into the cadavers of their victims. Afterwards, a good bath is necessary!

218-219
This young male has recently attained the age at which he will have to leave the pride. He will have to then procure his own food.

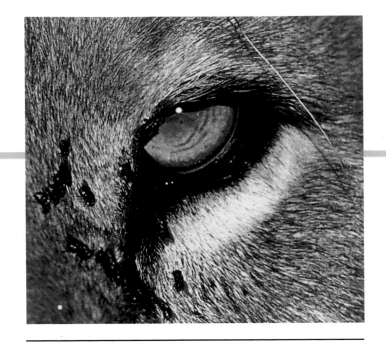

PHOTO CREDITS

All photographs are by Christine
and Michel Denis-Huot except for the following:
12-13 Lessing/Contrasto; *14 top* Archivio White Star;
14 bottom G. Dagli Orti, Paris; *15* University of Pennsylvania
Museum, Philadelphia; *16 top* Araldo De Luca/Archivio White
Star; *16 center* Araldo De Luca/Archivio White Star;
16 bottom left Araldo De Luca/Archivio White Star;
16-17 Araldo De Luca/Archivio White Star; *17 top right* Araldo
De Luca/Archivio White Star; *18* Archivio Scala;
19 top Archivio Scala; *19 bottom left* Archivio Scala;
20 Victoria & Albert Museum; *21* Corbis/Grazia Neri;
22 Lessing/Contrasto; *23 top* Archivio Scala/Art Resource; *23
bottom* Double's/ICP; *24 top left* Archivio Scala; *24 center*
Marcello Bertinetti/Archivio White Star;
24 top right Giulio Veggi/Archivio White Star;
24-25 Archivio Scala; *25 left* Massimo Borchi/Archivio White
Star; *25 right* Marcello Bertinetti/Archivio White Star;
26-27 Giorgio Oddi/Il Dagherrotipo; *27 top* Lucio Bracco/Il
Dagherrotipo; *27 bottom* Giovanni Rinaldi/Il Dagherrotipo;
28 top left Fototeca Storica Nazionale; *28 bottom* Roger
Viollet/Contrasto; *29 top* Roger Viollet/Contrasto;
29 bottom G. Dagli Orti, Paris;
30-31 The Art Archive; *32-33* Hulton Archive/Laura Ronchi;
33 top left Mary Evans Picture Library;
33 top right Agence photographique de la Réunion des Musées
Nationaux; *33 bottom* Topham/Double's/ICP;
34 top right Photos12; *34 top right* Photos12;
34-35 Roger Viollet/Contrasto;
35 top Roger Viollet/Contrasto

**The authors would like to thank all friends at Masai-Mara Reserve
for providing information and help.**

All photographs in the book have been taken with Canon EOS1N, EOS3, and EOS1V cameras;
Canon 600 F4, 500 F4 IS, 300 F2.8 IS objectives; 20-35, 28-70, and 70-200 zoom lens.
Color films by Fujichrome Provia and Sensia.